POLICY AND PRACTICE IN HEALTH AND SOCIAL CARE
NUMBER TWENTY-SEVEN

Homelessness, Social Exclusion and Health

Global perspectives, local solutions

CW01497028

POLICY AND PRACTICE IN HEALTH AND SOCIAL CARE

See www.dunedinacademicpress.co.uk for details of all our publications

POLICY AND PRACTICE IN HEALTH AND SOCIAL CARE

SERIES EDITORS

CHARLOTTE L. CLARKE AND CHARLOTTE PEARSON

Homelessness, Social Exclusion and Health
Global perspectives, local solutions

Fiona Cuthill

School of Health in Social Science, University of Edinburgh

EDINBURGH ◆ LONDON

First published in 2019 by Dunedin Academic Press Ltd.
Head Office: Hudson House, 8 Albany Street, Edinburgh EH1 3QB
London Office: 352 Cromwell Tower, Barbican, London EC2Y 8NB

ISBNs:
9781780460710 (Paperback)
9781780466286 (PDF)
9781780466040 (ePub)
9781780466057 (Kindle)

British Library Cataloguing in Publication Data
A catalogue record for this book is available from the British Library

Typeset by Makar Publishing Production, Edinburgh
Printed in Great Britain by CPI Antony Rowe

Mixed Sources
Product group from well-managed
forests and other controlled sources
www.fsc.org Cert no. TT-COC-2082
© 1996 Forest Stewardship Council
FSC

CONTENTS

ACKNOWLEDGEMENTS

My sincere thanks to everyone I have worked with over the years – both UK citizens and migrants – for sharing your life stories and experiences of homelessness with me. I will be forever grateful to you for your trust and generosity. Thank you to Anthony Kinahan, Director at Dunedin Academic Press, for your patience with missed deadlines and to Charlotte Clarke, Series Editor, for believing that I could finish this book and for persuading me to do so. Neil, Katy and Adam: your willingness to be involved in writing this book was invaluable. Thank you to my ever supportive family – Colin and the girls – for your continued encouragement and enthusiasm.

GLOSSARY OF ABBREVIATIONS

ACE	adverse childhood experience
ASPIRE	Analysing Safety and Place in Immigrant and Refugee Experience
B&B	bed and breakfast
BME	black and minority ethnic
CDC	Centers for Disease Control and Prevention
CHI	Centre for Homelessness Innovation
COSLA	Confederation of Scottish Local Authorities
CPR	cardiopulmonary resuscitation
DFT	Detained Fast Track
ECHR	European Convention of Human Rights
ETHOS	European Typology of Homelessness and Housing Exclusion
EU	European Union
FEANTSA	European Federation of National Organisations Working with the Homeless
GDP	gross domestic product
GHN	Glasgow Homeless Network
GLA	Greater London Authority
GP	general practice
HARSAG	Homeless and Rough Sleepers Action Group
HAS	Homeless Action Scotland
HIV	human immunodeficiency virus
HPSG	Homelessness Prevention Strategy Group
HSCP	Health and Social Care Partnership
JCHR	Joint Committee for Human Rights
LGBT	lesbian, gay, bisexual, and transgender
MDG	millennium development goals
MEH	multiple exclusion homelessness
NASS	National Asylum Support Service
NCD	noncommunicable disease

NGO	non-governmental organisation
NHS	National Health Service
NRPF	No Recourse to Public Funds
ORBITAL	Outcome Reporting in Brief Intervention Trials: Alcohol
ONS	Office of National Statistics
PAFRAS	Positive Action for Refugees and Asylum Seekers
PTSD	post-traumatic stress disorder
RV	recreational vehicle
ScotPHN	Scottish Public Health Network
SESPAS	Spanish Society of Public Health and Health Administration
PIE	psychologically informed environments
PTSD	post-traumatic stress disorder
SDG	sustainable development goals
SHORE	sustainable housing on release for everyone
SNP	Scottish National Party
SoE	State of Emergency
SPS	Scottish Prison Service
STI	sexually transmitted infection
TB	tuberculosis
UNDP	United Nations Development Plan
UNHCR	United Nations High Commission for Refugees
WHO	World Health Organization

CHAPTER 1

Framing homelessness: Strangers on the streets

The introduction sets out the direction of this book by contextualising the health of people who experience homelessness as the most severe in the social gradient of health within a world of widening health inequalities. This chapter starts by framing the lives of people who experience homelessness at the point where the pressures of globalisation and the local collide. As 'strangers on the streets', both the local citizen and the undocumented migrant are located as outsiders to society, both jostling for a space on the streets of the Global North in search of a 'home'. Homelessness, health and migration are defined and described.

An intersectional approach to homelessness and health

As dusk falls over the thriving cities of the Global North, the marble door-ways of international stores exchange the clip of designer heels for the scrape of cardboard 'mattresses'. The young person refused asylum, the undocumented migrant, the local citizen and the destitute of the city jostle for space, for a bed for the night, for a place to make sense of their lives: the shadow of their lives refracted through the glass displays of luxury goods. The winners and losers of global capitalism are juxtaposed in the same frame for another night. Our city streets become witness to 'the "lamentable sight" of homelessness on the one hand, and the spectacle of capital on the other' (Gerrard and Farrugia, 2015, p. 2220).

Contemporary urban spaces, once the domain of the local poor and marginalised, have become contested globalised places, where the displaced and destitute migrant finds him- or herself co-located with the local rough sleeper. Globalisation is lived out in the day-to-day experience of sharing doorways, sofas and urban public spaces as the undocumented migrant and the citizen both negotiate lives as 'strangers on the streets'. Both excluded multiple times from society and positioned as the 'other' (Said, 1979), rough sleepers exist as outsiders to society and migrants as cultural strangers to each other, often speaking different languages and observing divergent cultural norms. For the undocumented migrant, they are positioned as strangers through lack of citizenship rights, legal status, racism and cultural difference (Amin, 2012; 2013); for the citizen, it is largely through adverse childhood experiences, substance misuse, family breakdown and inadequate housing provision (Chamberlain and Johnson, 2013; Fitzpatrick *et al.*, 2011a). While a plethora of international literature testifies to the causes of homelessness for both groups (Bowpitt *et al.*, 2011; Fitzpatrick *et al.*, 2013; Guirguis-Younger *et al.*, 2014; Hyde, 2005; Roche, 2004), the academic study of homelessness as experienced by forced migrants and local citizens has been located in two distinct, but overlapping, bodies of research. Migrant homelessness is generally located within the field of refugee studies, while citizen homelessness is positioned within the fields of urban and housing studies. The literature in relation to the health needs of each group has developed in an equally divergent way: global public health scholars focus on the health of refugees as a subset of migrant health (Bradby *et al.*, 2015); the health of people seeking asylum and undocumented migrants is explored in relation to the different 'stages' of the refugee 'journey': leaving country of origin, border crossings and arrival (de Lima, 2017). In contrast, the public health literature in relation to citizen homelessness is located at the nexus of mental health, harmful substance use and multiple exclusion homelessness (MEH) (Kim *et al.*, 2010; Padgett *et al.*, 2006; Unger *et al.*, 1997), where migrant health is situated as a subgroup of the homeless population (Allan and Sakamoto, 2014).

The reality for many people who sleep on the streets of the Global North is of the undocumented migrant and the local citizen sharing the same doorways each night. Born on different sides of the globe, the lives of these outsiders meld together as they form friendships and learn to navigate the hazards of the city streets. Drawing on Amin's (2012) work critically analysing the politics of identity and intolerance that circulate towards migrants in a multicultural Europe, this unfolding story has only recently received scholarly attention as these two groups interact as 'strangers on the streets' (Darling, 2009), and yet their lives and health needs intersect as both forced migration and homelessness increase. As Tudor Hart (1972) asserted over four decades ago, there is still general agreement among those working and researching with people experiencing homelessness that those who are most excluded from society experience the greatest health needs and yet have the least access to services (Guirguis-Younger and McNeil, 2014; Pauly, 2014).

In the Global North, the sight of 'strangers on the streets' is becoming increasingly familiar: from the boats landing on the beaches of Lampedusa in Italy to the shopping trolleys negotiating the rough sleeper in doorways of luxury stores. And yet, despite the risks to health and well-being for both groups, the sight of people sleeping overnight on the streets engenders fear and hostility in many countries of the world. As I write, Hungary's ruling party, Fidesz, is amending the country's foundation law to criminalise homelessness. This would make it illegal for anyone to regularly reside in public spaces (Nicholls, 2018). Bauman (2017) argues that fear is the main driver for this:

> Strangers tend to cause anxiety precisely because of being 'strange' – and so, fearsomely unpredictable, unlike the people with whom we interact daily and from who we believe we know what to expect; for all we know, the massive influx of strangers might have destroyed the things we cherished – and intend to maim or wipe out our consolingly familiar way of life (Bauman, 2017, p. 8).

In framing people who experience homelessness as 'strangers on the streets', I am acknowledging the multiple ways that people can be treated as 'outsiders' to their family, community and society, and yet I also acknowledge that, in many ways, homelessness is becoming increasingly familiar. As more and more people are seen sleeping under the harsh winter weather conditions in the Global North, both the composition of people who are experiencing homelessness and the intensity of political debate is changing (Castles, 2017). Homelessness has shifted from a chronic, persistent low-grade societal problem to an issue of high political priority (Scottish Government, 2018a). Regular media stories of homelessness and pictures of rough sleepers building encampments in certain areas of cities, such as under bridges and pedestrian walkways, has increased visibility and intensified the debate around housing, health and the place of 'strangers on the streets' (Greenfeld, 2018).

Responses to these accounts are many: the global media is replete with stories of rough sleepers being swept from the streets of global cities in response to international sporting events: for example, the Beijing Olympics (Watts, 2008) and the Football World Cup in Russia (Stewart, 2018). The USA regularly operates 'sweeps', clearing areas of rough sleepers and moving them into designated areas in an attempt to maintain the aesthetic of the city for the middle class (Speer, 2018). In countries that have a more tolerant approach to rough sleeping, such as the UK and other countries of the European Union (EU), rough sleeping is provoking increased levels of discomfort from the public and policymakers, resulting in two different responses: firstly, the EU, UK and devolved governments of Scotland, Wales and Northern Ireland are working with non-governmental organisations (NGOs) to develop a range of different plans to end rough sleeping and to enable people to move from the streets into bricks-and-mortar accommodation (Crisis, 2018; Littlewood et al., 2017; Scottish Government, 2018a)l and, secondly, stories have emerged of increasingly coercive measures being used to remove rough sleepers from popular UK urban locales. Examples include authorities in Manchester putting spikes in places where rough sleepers sleep (Worley, 2017), moving on rough sleepers before the Royal Wedding in Windsor (Sherwood, 2018) and replacing public benches with 'homeless proof' alternatives in Birmingham (Baynes, 2018). Johnsen et al. (2018) have recently developed a typology of social control measures – both 'regulatory' and 'soft' measures – used to manage rough sleeping. In their paper, they identify the ways that force, coercion, bargaining, influence and tolerance are used in different contexts to manage the visibility of homeless lives. The sight of increasing numbers of rough sleepers, and the increased media and political interest in the lives of those who sleep on the streets, has caused critical scholars to caution that homelessness has become a discursive device created to be a 'social problem' to be fixed (Gerrard and Farrugia, 2015).

And yet, we cannot merely point the finger at media depictions or at hard-pressed municipal authorities as they balance the needs of business to attract shoppers and tourists into the city, while managing the needs of those who sleep on the streets. The visibility of 'strangers on the streets' demands a response from us too: to ignore, to give money, to abuse, to judge, to pity or to tolerate (Gerrard and Farrugia, 2015). As we gaze on pictures of bedraggled people in dirty sleeping bags or step over migrants asleep in doorways, a question is asked of us: where do we position ourselves and what do we see? As active citizens, and readers of this book, who do we identify with in these frames? The passer-by, situating the people in the picture as the 'scroungers' of society, passive recipients of our charity, pity or hate? Or do we identify with the person on the street – through acquaintance or through personal experience – remembering a time in life when we experienced homelessness ourselves? Or maybe we are the shop manager locking up for the night, annoyed that the glitter of the goods on sale will be dulled by the human display of desperation outside the window? Whatever our position, the scene demands a response; we are required to give an answer.

The answer presented in this book is to locate homelessness in the context of a rapidly changing world, where global forces exert local pressures as never before. Those who are vulnerable on the global stage become the displaced, the destitute and the disregarded on the local turf across a wide range of countries and context. Despite tough measures from policymakers and city governors over the years, particularly in North America where people who experience homelessness have been criminalised and removed from public spaces (Mitchell, 1997; 2003; Upton, 2016), homelessness remains persistent, and is increasing, in the urban spaces of the Global North. Wacquant (2007) conceptualises this driving of the poor into city ghetto spaces as 'territorial stigmatisation' in advanced capitalist economies. Despite increased efforts in the Global North to tackle homelessness, there are no easy fixes. The reasons that people find themselves homeless are multiple, structural, individual and complex: a collision of global forces and adverse life experiences in childhood that are played out over the life course (Fitzpatrick et al., 2011a; Guirguis-Younger et al., 2014). While charities might assert that we are 'all two pay cheques away from homelessness', homelessness is experienced disproportionately by those who live fragile lives, have experienced adverse life experiences and live in poverty (Bramley and Fitzpatrick, 2018).

The aim of this book is to explore homelessness and health within the context of the contemporary global world, and to add to the growing body of work that recognises the need to understand homelessness and health as a complex interplay between the consequence of pressures in a global capitalist economy, the outcomes of local policies and the result of individual behaviours. The experience of homelessness does not discriminate on the basis of race, culture, gender, age or sexuality, and an intersectional approach to homelessness is taken where the health of migrants who experience homelessness is not considered as a subset of the topic but as integrated in the field of study. In addition, some of the intersections of sexuality, gender, youth, old age, ethnicity, disability and homelessness will be highlighted along the way.

Linking homelessness and health

Homelessness and health are inextricably linked: having a good house provides not only shelter, warmth and protection, but also a sense of identity, security and being 'at home' in the world (Mallett, 2004; Padgett, 2007; Saunders and Williams, 1988; Somerville, 1992). Hewett and Halligan (2010) assert that homelessness is a health care issue and that good housing is a prerequisite for health: the Scottish Public Health Network (ScotPHN) emphasises the need for safe, dry, affordable and appropriate housing to give the best opportunities for educational attainment, for relationships to thrive and for sustainable neighbourhoods to flourish (Tweed et al., 2017). In addition, the authors emphasise the important role of good housing, safe and green public spaces, a strong local economy, good transport links and infrastructure to enable strong social relationships and health and well-being to flourish in communities. Overcrowded, temporary and damp housing as well as fuel poverty expose people to stress, anxiety and respiratory disease (Braubach and Fairburn, 2010). Insecure housing and frequent moves from temporary accommodation can create a disconnect from family and community, causing stress and anxiety and low educational attainment for children. For those who sleep on the streets, the risks of poor health and death are the most severe (Fazel et al., 2014; Homeless Link, 2015). While rough sleeping is the visible 'face' of poverty, and often used as a shortcut for homelessness, it is recognised as only a small part of the homelessness puzzle; most homelessness is experienced as overcrowded accommodation, hostels, temporary supported accommodation, sofa-surfing and shelters (Fitzpatrick et al., 2018b; FEANTSA and the Fondation Abbé Pierre, 2018).

Defining homelessness is notoriously difficult and comparison of data between different countries is problematic as definitions of homelessness range from rough sleeping and hostel accommodation to those who are in settled but overcrowded buildings. Research agendas increasingly seek to conceptualise and measure homelessness across the Global South, as well as the Global North (Busch-Geertsema *et al.*, 2016), although data collection systems are inconsistent (Busch-Geertsema *et al.*, 2014). In this book, a broad definition of homelessness is used to include a range of different fragile housing environments and to understand homelessness beyond the narrow definition of rough sleeping. The highly respected *Homelessness Monitor* report (Fitzpatrick *et al.*, 2018b) definition of homelessness is used to define homelessness. This includes the following homeless groups:

- people sleeping rough;
- single homeless people living in hostels, shelters and temporary supported accommodation;
- statutorily homeless households – that is, households who seek housing assistance from local authorities on grounds of being currently or imminently without accommodation;
- 'hidden homeless' households – that is, people who may be considered homeless but whose situation is not 'visible' either on the streets or in official statistics. Classic examples would include households living in severely overcrowded conditions, squatters, people 'sofa-surfing' around friends' or relatives' homes, those involuntarily sharing with other households on a long-term basis, and people sleeping rough in hidden locations' (Fitzpatrick *et al.*, 2018b, p. 1).

Another very useful typology of homelessness and housing exclusion is the European Typology of Homelessness and Housing Exclusion (ETHOS) and is provided by FEANTSA (European Federation of organisations working with the people who are homeless) (FEANTSA, 2005). Rooflessness, houselessness, insecure housing and inadequate housing are all identified as constituting homelessness, and these conceptual categories are then divided into thirteen different experiences of people who are living:

- rough;
- in emergency accommodation;
- in accommodation for the homeless;
- in a women's shelter;

- in accommodation for immigrants;
- due to be released from institutions;
- in longer-term support due to homelessness;
- in insecure accommodation;
- under threat of eviction;
- under threat of violence;
- in temporary/non-conventional structures;
- unfit housing;
- in extreme overcrowding.

This typology broadens out the concept of homelessness to include understandings of 'home' as much more than merely a roof over one's head.

It is clear that homelessness is a category that has been built on shifting sands, and terminology has powerful implications, as people experience homelessness and organisations struggle to ensure that they are present in policy decisions (Watson, 2000). Discursive constitutions of 'the homeless' and of people seeking asylum and refugees are powerful (Gabrielatos and Baker, 2008), and the representation of refugee lives shape the ways that the lives of people experiencing homelessness are constructed and the services that they receive (Renedo and Jovchelovitch, 2007). In general, the policy language of homelessness in the UK is focused on those who are eligible to be registered with the local authorities as statutory homeless, but this obscures the fact that many people who experience homelessness are not eligible to be registered in this way: those who exit the asylum system following a refused claim; those with No Recourse to Public Funds (NRPF); and those who choose not to register because they do not want to alert authorities of their migrant status or because of negative experiences of statutory services in the past.

This book defines refugees and asylum seekers according to the legal definitions adopted by the UK government in accordance with its obligations as signatory of the 1951 Refugee Convention and its 1967 Protocol. According to these definitions, a refugee is:

> A person who owing to a well-founded fear of being persecuted for reasons of race, religion, nationality, membership of a particular social group, or political opinion is outside the country of his nationality, and is unable to or, owing to such fear, is unwilling to avail himself of the protection of that country.

An asylum seeker is someone who is part of the ongoing legal process and awaiting an outcome, having lodged an application for protection on the basis of the Refugee Convention (or Article 3 of the European Convention of Human Rights).

The terminology used to describe forced migrants is politically charged and words are powerful to shape perceptions. In this book, undocumented migrants will be the terminology used to refer to a wide range of people including students and tourists who have overstayed their visas, people who are refused asylum, trafficked people and anyone who does not have a right to residence in a country. This can include people who entered the UK legally but have lost their right of residence or who have entered the UK illegally and do not have the right of residence.

It is useful to note that the terminology for homelessness for migrants in the UK is usually expressed in terms of 'destitution', rather than homelessness, as this is the commonly used term in government policy on migration. According to Section 95(3) of the Immigration and Asylum Act 1999:

> A person is destitute if he does not have adequate accommodation or any means of obtaining it (whether or not his other essential living needs are met); or he has adequate accommodation or the means of obtaining it but cannot meet his other essential living needs (Immigration and Asylum Act, 1999, p. 23).

The advantage of using the term 'destitution' is that it allows for a common definition within migrant studies and enables comparison across countries and regions (Allsopp et al., 2014). Some studies into destitution and asylum seekers have used this definition for destitution to argue that people who are supported by the state under the National Asylum Support Service (NASS) and are living on £37.75 per week are destitute as this is not adequate to meet essential living needs, even if they have accommodation (Refugee Action, 2006; Crawley et al., 2011; Allsopp et al., 2014). This definition locates people who are destitute as having accommodation but not enough money to adequately live. Fitzpatrick et al. (2018a) recently looked at factors pushing people into destitution and found that 1.5 million people were living in destitution in the UK in 2017 and, of those, 25% were born outside the country. Five in twelve of the migrants they interviewed had slept rough in the previous year. Cuts to benefits, sanctions on Universal Credit and debt were the most common causes of destitution in their study.

Bradby *et al.* (2017) suggest that we live in a world of superdiversity and, drawing on this and in considering citizen and migrant homelessness together, the term 'people experiencing homelessness' will be used in this book as a means of focusing on the experience of homelessness, rather than the policy or legal status of a person as either 'homeless' or 'destitute'. This includes: people who are undocumented migrants and have not applied for asylum; people who are awaiting forcible removal; those who have had a refused asylum application and subsequent appeal; and people who are stranded in the UK, as it is not safe to return to their home country (Anderson *et al.*, 2013; Allsopp *et al.*, 2014). The stories of both Alesky and Ahmed help to illustrate these lived experiences of homelessness for migrants hidden from view. (All names used as lived-experience examples are pseudonyms and anonymised.)

Lived experience: Alesky

I met Alesky during a research study in 2017, when he told me about his health needs and his 'choice' to live up a tree in a makeshift shelter he had made in a Scottish city. He explained that he had come to the UK from a eastern European country as a seasonal fruit picker a few years ago but that 'things had got difficult' and that he had experienced multiple difficulties. He had lost his passport as it was stolen from his bed and breakfast (B&B) accommodation, and when the fruit picking came to an end he had found it hard to find another job, and as he had no passport he couldn't prove eligibility to work. He didn't have enough money to apply for a new passport as he had been struggling for money and sleeping with friends. He started drinking alcohol to harmful levels to cope with the stress, and although he was now seeking help from the general practitioner (GP) he preferred to stay in the tree where he felt safe and secure. Alesky was very fearful of being found by the police as he was sure he would be detained and sent back to his country. He wanted to stay in the UK and to work, but his harmful alcohol use was now problematic and so he chose to stay living in the tree.

Lived experience: Ahmed

Likewise, Ahmed has lived for ten years destitute in a northern city in the UK since his appeal for asylum was refused in 2008. Having fled the civil war in Sudan in 2005, he arrived in the UK with a forged passport and without any official documentation detailing his torture in a Sudanese prison for allegedly being part of a political opposition group. Unable to 'prove' his refugee credentials, his claim for asylum had been refused and, terrified that if he went back to Sudan he would be imprisoned and tortured again, he now negotiates a life of homelessness by relying on the hospitality of friends, charity food banks and community meals. Ahmed argues that he is unable to obtain the necessary documentation to 'prove' his risk of persecution if he returns to Sudan but is too afraid to return home. Caught between 'Destitution and a Hard Place' (Cuthill *et al.*, 2013), he lives in a precarious life hidden from view.

Alesky and Ahmed's stories are not unique, nor are they new: scholars and human rights organisations have been highlighting the plight of those who live hidden lives of homelessness for the last two decades (Crawley *et al.*, 2011; Cuthill *et al.*, 2013; H. Lewis, 2007), but the government denies their existence and the focus remains on those who sleep rough in visible spaces on our streets. As Wright (1997, p. 1) asserts, 'homeless bodies, poor bodies, visible to passers-by, visible to the streets are open to the public's gaze, to the gaze of authority'. Often positioned as 'deviant' (Bradley-Engen, 2011), the experiences of stigma associated with homelessness are often conflated with other conditions such as harmful substance use, human immunodeficiency virus (HIV) and sexually transmitted infections (STIs) (Pauly, 2014; Wolitski *et al.*, 2009). Visibility is a choice, and for many people they choose not to be subject to that gaze. Nonetheless, their experience of homelessness is very real.

Homelessness is not only an experience, it is also an identity that is conferred – often by a powerful media – or an identity claimed by organisations or groups in order to secure funding or to access services. In this respect, it is important to name, and interrogate, the label of 'homeless' itself; at once a grouping and an exclusionary mechanism. One thing that scholars do largely agree on is that 'homeless identity is influenced by day-to-day lives that are on public display' (Parsell, 2011, p. 442). While recognising that the label 'homeless' can be actively used by individuals and organisations as an identity, it can also be a label that is conferred by society. Parsell's (2010) study of people experiencing homelessness in Brisbane, Australia – titled 'Homeless is what I am, not who I am' – foregrounds homelessness as an experience rather than an identity. It is all too common to read reports on 'the homeless', situating an experience as a 'label'. Scholars often conflate homelessness with rough sleeping and associated drug use: for example, Langegger and Koester (2017) explore poverty management in Denver and homeless citizens in ethnographic research and yet their research focuses on homeless injecting drug users. In order to guard against stigmatising language, homelessness is framed in this book as an experience, rather than a label, although it is recognised that in public health debates and in policy documents homelessness is often referred to as a grouping of the population.

Poverty, health inequalities and homelessness

Homelessness and health research, policy and practice are intertwined in the interactions of an advanced global economy. Homelessness is embedded in relationships of privilege and power, and while not denying the impact of trauma and adverse childhood experiences (ACEs) on later life (Bellis *et al.*, 2013; Coupar and Mackie, 2016) it is often pathologised and reduced to the frame of the individual or the local citizen. Despite a substantial volume of research evidence that highlights the importance of 'upstream' determinants of health, such as education, unemployment and other material and structural factors, Garthwaite *et al.* (2016) found that there was broad agreement among public health researchers that failure in policy to reduce health inequalities reflects a policy preoccupation with trying to change people's behaviours (improving diets, reducing alcohol intake, etc.). Research claims that policy interventions aimed only at behavioural level are unlikely to be effective in reducing health inequalities (Scott *et al.*, 2013) and could, in fact, exacerbate them (Whitehead, 2007). This is also seen in the homelessness and health literature, where homelessness is commonly conceptualised as a 'risk-factor' for ill health, and individual factors such as mental ill health, ACEs, domestic violence, looked-after children, criminal activity and harmful substance use have become the dominant narrative (Cronley, 2010).

'The homeless' are regularly grouped together as a subcategory of the population who live on the streets, rather than as a wide range of individuals who share the experience of living, or having lived, without a home. To be homeless is individualised, and newspaper headlines frequently run with stories of the 'unlucky' person who managed to 'escape' homelessness by their own efforts – and support of others – to 'turn their lives around' and lead a 'normal' life. A typical example is a recent story in the *Yorkshire Post*, which explained how Martha Hayward 'escaped a turbulent home life' and 'found herself homeless at the age of just sixteen'. It goes on to report:

> despite the poverty and drug addiction surrounding her, she defied all expectations to become a professional soprano. Now, a music teacher, she is determined to do what she can to help others (Yorkshire Post, 2017).

The discourse running through this article is of personal persistence over adversity.

While these stories are undoubtedly individually inspiring, they run the risk of placing the responsibility of entering and exiting homelessness squarely at the feet of those who experience homelessness and focus on individual behaviours, while drawing attention away from the structural causes of homelessness. The search for the causes of homelessness are polarised into those of individual responsibility or structural inequality, and while these polarisations have been strongly critiqued (Fitzpatrick, 2005) a moral judgement is often made on the people experiencing homelessness and the implicit implication is that it is within everyone's gift to be able to use individual effort and perseverance to exit homelessness. As Bauman (2017, p. 17) asserts: 'It is a human-all-too-human-habit to blame and punish the messengers for the hateful content of the message they are carrying'. The moral judgements that are made by society on people who experience homelessness is clearly articulated by Gowan (2010) in her illuminating ethnographic research with homeless people in San Francisco, where she identified the politicisation of homelessness as a moral failure in three different ways: as 'sin talk' – a pathological condition; as 'sick talk' – as a pathology; or as 'system talk' – structural inequality. In identifying these political discourses, Gowan (2010) not only articulated the narratives that persist in society but she also challenged the discourses of vulnerability that run through much of the research on homelessness. In identifying the ways that agency and resilience were demonstrated through the lives of people experiencing homelessness, she foregrounded the multiple ways that identity was forged on the streets. Nonetheless, these accounts are rare within health research and the moral capability and/or pathological explanations of homelessness appear to take centre stage. Individual experiences are embedded within the structures of local communities, national organisations and global relationships, and increasingly relate to our local lives, as globalisation is not only altering the world 'out there' but distant events are shaping our communities and impacting individual lives (Giddens, 2018). This is particularly so for those who live precarious lives of poverty and marginalisation.

Poverty has long been understood to be a pervasive factor for those experiencing homelessness, and living in poverty is more likely to result in episodes of homelessness. Sir Michael Marmot, international scholar on health inequalities, analysed the relationship between wealth, poverty and health, and he explained the social gradient in health, which he described as: 'a graded association between an individual's position on the social hierarchy and health: the lower the socioeconomic position of an individual, the worse their health' (Marmot, 2017a). He went on to explain how the social gradient reaches to the very top of the social ladder and to the very bottom, and that certain groups appear to not even be on the ladder: the socially excluded; people who find themselves homeless; those destitute following the asylum process; undocumented migrants; people experiencing harmful substance use; sex workers; and ex-prisoners. As the UK recognises the many achievements of seventy years of the National Health Service (NHS), where healthcare remains free at the point of delivery, it is of great concern that the 'health gap' (Marmot, 2015b) between the lives of the richest and the poorest in the UK remains evident and is widening. Mackenbach (2016) in a comparative European study has recently suggested that persistent health inequalities are an unwanted consequence of the modern welfare state.

In the most recent systematic review by Aldridge *et al.* (2017) into health inequalities, mortality rates for men in the most deprived areas of England and Wales are 2.8 times higher than people in the least deprived areas; the figures for women are 2.1 times higher. While these are depressing statistics, the figures for those who are socially excluded is dramatic: men who are socially excluded are nearly eight times more likely to die early than the average. For women, the figures are even more worrying: they are twelve times more likely to die than the average for women (Aldridge *et al.*, 2017). As Sir Michael Marmot so succinctly states:

> The challenge is to bring socially excluded populations in from the cold – literally and metaphorically – and to provide them with the opportunity to be part of a diverse and flourishing society (Marmot, 2017a).

The influential 'Hard edges' report (Bramley *et al.*, 2015) mapped severe and multiple disadvantage in England and found that poor white men, aged 25–44, with a history of childhood adversity, trauma and social exclusion were the most disadvantaged in society. At least 250,000 people had contact with substance misuse, criminal justice and/or homelessness services. International research has described high mortality rates for a range of people who inhabit the margins of society (Morrison, 2009): those who experience harmful substance use (Arendt *et al.*, 2011) and those who are imprisoned (Nielsen *et al.*, 2011) in Denmark and prisoners in Scotland (Graham *et al.*, 2015). Homelessness is seen within the health literature as a 'late marker' of severe and complex disadvantage (McDonagh, 2011) and the result of health and social inequities (Hetherington and Hamlet, 2015). The health of rough sleepers represents visually the most extreme end of health inequalities that we know exist both between and within countries. The health needs of individuals are shaped by the pathways they experience into homelessness, depending on a range of adverse life experiences (Chamberlain and Johnson, 2013; Fitzpatrick *et al.*, 2013), gender (Tutty *et al.*, 2013) or age (Morris *et al.*, 2005), and are impacted by the global, national and local policies that contribute to housing tenure.

The health and well-being outcomes of people who are homeless are inextricably linked: rough sleepers experience poorer physical and mental health outcomes than the general population (Fazel *et al.*, 2005; Fazel *et al.*, 2014; Breedvelt, 2016), die in middle-age (Crisis, 2011) and are less likely to benefit from health improvement interventions (Aldridge *et al.*, 2017; Story *et al.*, 2014). In fact, the health outcomes for the poorest people in the UK 'can appear to be on a different scale to the rest of society' (Marmot, 2017b, p. 186). Fazel *et al.* (2014) reviewed the existing international epidemiological literature on health and homelessness in high-income countries, and their findings are very instructive here. The authors detail a range of physical and mental ill health experienced by people who are homeless, including high prevalence rates of infectious diseases, such as HIV, tuberculosis (TB) and hepatitis C, and higher rates of psychiatric disorders and harmful alcohol and drug use. They also note that there are higher rates of unintentional injury and suicide among people experiencing homelessness (Cohen, 2008). In addition, the homeless population is ageing, and with this comes increased chronic disease, such as hypertension and cardiovascular disease, and cognitive impairment.

For those sleeping on the streets with the most complex health and social care needs, scholars have identified this as experiencing MEH (Carter, 2007: Fitzpatrick *et al.*, 2011b; Fitzpatrick *et al.*, 2013). The criteria for MEH is usually an experience of rough sleeping, living in insecure accommodation or squatting and an indicator of 'deep exclusion' (Bowpitt *et al.*, 2011). This group is often associated with harmful substance use, mental ill health and increasing hospital admissions. Although not the original intention, in everyday health and social care practice the label MEH has become a shorthand for people who led 'chaotic lives' (MEAM, 2009, p. 8). While MEH is the terminology of choice for academia, health and social care practice, the stigma of homelessness remains high and narratives of the 'underserving poor', 'the scrounger', 'the addict' remain strong. Contrary to popular narratives that people who live on the streets perpetrate violence, third-sector organisations have recently reported that violence is more frequently perpetrated against rough sleepers than by them, and instances of brain injuries are high. Migrants, especially homeless migrants, are particularly vulnerable to exploitation and abuse. Positioned in the lowest rungs of society:

> migrants stand for that sought-after bottom located even farther down – beneath the bottom to which the indigenous *miserable* have been consigned and committed; a bottom that may render one's own lot a little bit less bitter, unendurable and intolerable (Bauman, 2017, p. 14).

With NRPF, they are often forced into illegal work and risk accident, injury and exploitation (Dwyer *et al.*, 2011; Lewis *et al.*, 2014). It is not uncommon to walk around the cities of the UK and see people begging on the streets with signs that state: 'I am Scottish [English/Welsh] and in need.' Differentiating themselves from the migrant homeless, people on the streets implicitly assert that they are more 'deserving' of the coins thrown from the pockets of the passer-by. Lancione's (2011) doctoral research in Turin likewise demonstrated how Italians experiencing homelessness differentiated themselves from migrants on the streets to assert their self-worth.

The healthcare needs of migrants are both similar, and different, to the local populations, where psychological trauma related to torture, rape, bereavement, loss and persecution are evident for people seeking asylum

(Gerritsen *et al.*, 2006; Hermansson *et al.*, 2003); ACEs are strongly associated with MEH for the citizen population (Bellis *et al.*, 2013; Coupar and Mackie, 2016). In research examining the experience of homelessness with migrants in the UK in 2012, Fitzpatrick *et al.* (2012) found that non-migrants who were homeless experienced higher levels of violence, suicide and self-harm. In addition, the authors identified the indicators of MEH – harmful substance use, street culture and institutional care – as more prevalent for non-migrants than migrants. For the majority of participants in their study, homelessness was experienced by migrants for the first time while in the UK. Nonetheless, when the toll of destitution manifests itself, barriers between the migrant and the local citizen dissolve and they are both exposed to the same physical and psychological impacts of homelessness and rough sleeping. Access to services is problematic: for the MEH it is through lack of specialist provision, services that are not flexible to understandings of trauma and fear and anxiety around statutory services (Johnson, 2015); for the person experiencing homelessness following the asylum process it is through charges for health services, fear of detention in an increasingly 'hostile environment' in the UK (Travis, 2013), where the Home Office has been accused of using data from third-sector organisations to track and remove homeless migrants and through cultural/language difficulties. Levels of fear and anxiety run high, compounding existing mental health issues and past psychological trauma. In this environment, people are afraid to access statutory services, and health needs are often ignored until a crisis occurs (Crawley *et al.*, 2011; Cuthill *et al.*, 2013; Lewis, 2007).

Concern with the high mortality and morbidity rates for people who experience homelessness is not only a concern to healthcare providers and practitioners but also to economists and policymakers. The estimated healthcare costs incurred by people who are homeless vary, but an assessment by the Department of Health in England in 2010 stated that healthcare costs ascribed to homeless people was at least £85 million per year. This was calculated as approximately eight times greater than those of similar aged adults. In addition, length of stay in hospital was three times longer than those of the general population of a similar age (Department of Health, 2010).

Homelessness in the Global North

In the Global North, homelessness – particularly rough sleeping – has been on the increase and is now termed at 'crisis levels' by activists in the USA, Europe and Australia. In the USA there is an annual count of people who are 'rough sleepers' on one night each year, and in 2016 there was an increase of 1% in recorded numbers of 'rough sleepers', to 553,742 people (US Department of Housing and Urban Development, 2017). Los Angeles recorded the most people sleeping rough at 55,000, with increases also noted in many other cities including New York. In Europe, the European Federation of National Organisations Working with the Homeless states that the social crisis in housing in Europe is worsening and the number of homeless or displaced people in Europe has grown over the last four years (FEANTSA and the Fondation Abbé Pierre, 2018). Since 2010, every country in Europe – with the exception of Finland and Norway – has seen a dramatic increase in the number of people experiencing homelessness. The highest increase of rough sleepers in the EU region is in England, where a 169% rise was recorded between 2010 and 2016 (Fitzpatrick *et al.*, 2018b). Likewise, in Germany, a 150% increase was seen between 2014 and 2017 (FEANTSA and the Fondation Abbé Pierre, 2018). In Australia, the difference in the numbers of people as recorded as homeless in the 2011 and the 2016 national census rose by 14% (Australian Bureau of Statistics, 2018), and all of these increases are seen in countries that have experienced steady economic growth over the same time period.

While these figures of absolute numbers of rough sleepers tell a worrying story, drilling down into the data also uncovers the changing and unequal structural issues driving homelessness. The one-night street count in the USA in the winter of 2017/18 revealed that there was a shift away from people sleeping in shelters and an increase in people living in doorways, tents and vans (US Department of Housing and Urban Development, 2017; Watkin, 2013). Underlying the statistics in these studies in the USA, Europe and Australia is the disproportionate numbers of people who are from black and minority ethnic groups (BME) living on the streets: in the USA, African–Americans make up more than one-third of the number of rough sleepers (US Department of Housing and Urban Development, 2017); in Australia, the census data reveals that, while only 28.2% of Australians are immigrants, 45% of people experiencing homelessness are immigrants. In addition, while 2.8% of Australians are Aboriginal or Torres

Strait Islanders, they make up 20% of the homeless population (Australian Bureau of Statistics, 2018). In Germany, authors of the FEANTSA and the Fondation Abbé Pierre (2018) study note that refugees have been included in the homelessness statistics for the first time, and this accounts for the increase in homelessness in Germany.

While the FEANTSA and the Fondation Abbé Pierre (2018) report stated that the whole of Europe was in a housing crisis and urged increased measures to tackle homelessness, there have been successes: Finland have successfully reduced homelessness, almost to the point of eradication (Pleace, 2017). This was achieved through a combination of permanent housing provision with needs-based support, known as Housing First, and coordinated action between the state, municipalities and the third sector. While the reduction in the number of people sleeping rough is an admirable goal, it is only the tip of the iceberg in terms of the number of people experiencing homelessness. During the winter of 2017/18 in Scotland, 80–120 people were estimated to be sleeping 'rough' on the streets of Edinburgh, while 34,972 homelessness applications were submitted across Scotland (Scottish Government, 2018d). If rough sleeping is the visible manifestation of poverty and global displacement in a global capitalist economy, then it should not obscure the scale of homelessness that is hidden and out of public sight: people living in unstable housing, overcrowding, sofa-surfing and a range of other fragile housing conditions.

In Scotland, we benefit from strong policy mandates that frame homelessness within a human rights approach to health (NHS Health Scotland, 2016a), where homelessness is described in policy terms as unfair, unjust and preventable (NHS Health Scotland, 2016b) and the statutory responsibility of public bodies. Within this framework, health is understood to be a right for everyone to the highest attainable standard – as recognised within the European Convention on Economic Social and Cultural Rights – and should be equally available and accessible to all, irrespective of housing status. The focus of resources is on the people who need most support to enable them to be full participants in economic, cultural and social society.

Overall, the number of people who apply for, and are registered as, statutory homeless has fallen steadily in Scotland since the peak of 57,672 in 2008/09 (Scottish Government, 2018d). This is largely attributed to the implementation of housing options in 2010 (Scottish

Housing Register, 2014). In 2017/18, however, there was a 1% increase in homeless applications recorded, at 34,972 (National Statistics for Scotland, 2018). In addition, the number of applications in 2017/18 increased in seventeen out of thirty-two local authorities in Scotland. Shelter, one of the national homelessness charities in the UK, estimates that 5,000 people sleep rough over the year in Scotland and asserts that there has been a 10% increase in street sleeping in 2017/18. Of particular note are the increasing numbers of people who register as statutory homeless in Scotland from private rented accommodation. In Scotland in 2015, 61% of households were owner occupier, 23% renting from social landlords and 14% in private rented accommodation (Scottish Government, 2016a).

Undocumented migrants and people who experience homelessness following the asylum system do not feature on statutory homelessness figures and are termed as having NRPF. This means that they are not allowed to work and yet have no entitlement to welfare support, relying on friends and third-sector organisations for food and shelter for the night. If this fails, they can find themselves sleeping on the streets but often hidden from view. Recently, a coalition of charities and campaigning organisations, including Amnesty International, ran a campaign called 'Still Human; Still Here' (2013; 2017) to highlight the invisibility in policy and practice of undocumented migrants, and the reality of their homeless experience. Increasingly, researchers and campaigners in the third sector are calling for a recognition of the 'hidden homeless' – those who fall under definitions of homelessness but are not recognised in policy or official government figures. Nonetheless, the 'hidden homeless' access health and well-being services and live the most precarious of lives.

An intersectional approach to homelessness

While it is widely acknowledged that there is a high prevalence of harmful alcohol and drug use in people who experience homelessness (Bramley *et al.*, 2015), it is not enough to consider health and homelessness only in relation to the local male alcoholic rough sleeper. Increasingly, health outcomes are recognised as being shaped by the multiple intersections of gender, race, culture, disability, sexuality and identity. Indeed, public health scholars are calling for the concept of intersectionality to be used in all public health research in order to develop more nuanced understandings of the different ways that women, migrants, gypsies and travellers, sex workers, young people, people with disabilities and the elderly experience health and well-being while homeless (Kapilashrami *et al.*, 2015; Mayock and Sheridan, 2012). The intersectional literature is also uncovering the multiple ways that stigma and racism impact negatively on health and well-being (Viruell-Fuentes *et al.*, 2012).

Representation of social experiences

As homelessness becomes increasingly a named structure – a way of representing social experience – it also becomes validated and embedded in society. Parsell (2011, p. 442) warns that the people we refer to as 'homeless people' have become known 'through derogatory representations, they have been portrayed as the embodiment of the negative identity they have been ascribed'. The danger of a book on homelessness and health is that the very category of homelessness becomes increasingly recognised and authorised by those who sit beyond the experience. This authorial position is driven largely by – very understandable – policy agendas to end homelessness, but risks positioning homelessness outside the functioning of a global social world (Farrugia and Gerrard, 2016). The core tension at the heart of the debate is the need to name the category of 'homelessness', while understanding that it is a socially constructed entity. As Bourdieu (1991, p. 105) notes: '[T]he act of naming helps to establish the structure of this world, and does so all the more significantly the more widely it is recognized, that is, authorized.'

I am acutely aware that, in writing a book on homelessness and health, I contribute to the authorisation of the experience of homelessness from the comfort of the academy and my housed 'armchair'. I collude in Bourdieu's (1991) 'naming' and 'establishing' homelessness as a category of people to be placed under the microscope; to be examined and poked and prodded to uncover their flaws. Having worked as a nurse with people who experience homelessness for more than fifteen years, and having conducted participatory research with people who have been through the refugee journey ending in destitution, I understand the importance of professional power relationships. As Farrugia and Gerrard (2016) warn:

> The act of naming, identifying, describing, counting and measuring the disadvantaged, poor or marginalised 'other' reveals much

about normative understandings and assumptions, about what it is to be 'mainstream', 'successful', 'typical', and acts of recognition within academic research create power relationships between academic subjects and research objects (Farrugia and Gerrard, 2016, p. 268).

Like many people researching and writing in the field of homelessness, I am driven by a strong sense of social justice and a drive to influence policy to end homelessness (Fitzpatrick *et al.*, 2000), and yet I oscillate between two standpoints: not wanting to collude with the powerful authorial position of the housed academic in naming and reifying the 'homeless' subject and yet also wishing to explore and illuminate the field of homelessness and health for students, scholars, colleagues, policymakers and healthcare practitioners. The writing of this book brings a genuine desire to draw attention to migrant and citizen homelessness together in one text and to highlight the health needs of people who experience homelessness. In doing so, I aim to contribute to the alleviation of homelessness is some way, but this book also comes with a declaration of my own limited view of the field: as a scholar, a healthcare professional and as someone who has no lived experience of homelessness.

I have worked for many years as a community nurse with people who are destitute following the asylum process in the UK, people who are homeless citizens, homeless migrant workers and undocumented migrants, and, while I come to this book with a scholar's head and a humanitarian heart, my view is obscured by the power and privilege that I enjoy. I understand homelessness as an object of knowledge, rather than of experience; and, by presenting issues of homelessness and health as a policy problem to be solved (Bacchi, 2009), I am part of the system I critique.

In foregrounding the voice of those who have lived experience of homelessness, both local citizens and migrants, lived-experience examples and narratives are widely used throughout this book to bring the voices of those who live with homelessness to the page and to bring the empirical studies to life. These have been collected while writing this book, from people I have met while working in a voluntary capacity with homeless organisations, during research studies I have conducted and as a nurse consultant in the local NHS. All the names and identities of the participants have been changed to protect anonymity, and permission has been given by all participants to include the stories they told me in research studies or in this book.

Outline of the book

Grounded in more than two decades of research, this book explores the relationship between homelessness, health and a global capitalist economy. In response to Pleace's (1998) argument that homelessness research is too focused around the object of 'the homeless', rather than the wider social context of neoliberalism, this book explores the experience of homelessness, and resulting health implications, within a global political context. Drawing on interdisciplinary research linking social exclusion, health and well-being – the fields of sociology, politics and urban studies have been instructive here – this book argues that the experience of homelessness is most fully understood within the context of a rapidly globalising world, where migrant and citizen homelessness are positioned within the same frame. Moving from the global picture to the individual experience, each chapter opens the reader up to different aspects of migrant and citizen health and offers some examples of local solutions to difficult health issues. While the book has a global outlook, the policy and practice solutions are focused locally in Scotland, where a range of different projects, policies and community initiatives to improve health are highlighted.

Taking up the challenge of a global perspective, Chapter 2 focuses on the ways that the health of people who sleep on the streets is a microcosm of global health inequalities. As late modernity is marked by increasing mobility (Urry, 2007), Bauman (2007) asserts that this liquid modernity creates the conditions for the production of difference, where communities erect barriers to outsiders and those who are 'in' and those who are 'out' are clearly demarcated. Glocalisation, where the global and the local merge, is increasingly a feature of the twenty-first century and the health and well-being of communities is inextricably shaped by these wider forces exerting influence on local lives (O'Neill, 2010). The health and well-being of people who experience homelessness is located within the shifting boundaries of the 'asylum-migration' nexus (Castles, 2003), and citizen and migrant homelessness and health are brought together in Chapter 3.

In Chapter 4, I draw on scholars beyond the field of health and well-being to document the ways that people who live without safety and shelter – both citizens and migrants – find the strength to survive in the harshest of circumstances. I argue that there is a need for policymakers, healthcare practitioners and health scholars to move beyond the dominant discourse of illness, vulnerability and brokenness to include a discussion on resilience and resistance. While scholars in the field of urban geography have developed a strong analysis of agency and the 'performance' of homelessness enacted by those sleeping rough in our city streets, this approach has only recently been considered within the health literature to explore resilience and resistance as an asset for health and well-being. Certainly, many scholars see people who are seeking asylum and refugees as resilient, but, again, this approach has only started to filter into the health literature around the needs of migrants who experience homelessness.

Public health approaches to homelessness have gained traction in Scotland in recent years, and Neil Hamlet and Katy Hetherington take a public health approach to homelessness in Chapter 5, situating their work in the current policy context of Scotland. They draw on the exciting attempt currently underway in Scotland to end rough sleeping and to assess the impact of several initiatives on health and well-being.

Chapter 6 begins with a consideration of MEH and a critical exploration of 'pathways' into, and out of, homelessness. Individual and family factors such as harmful substance use, family breakdown, ACEs, interpersonal violence and mental ill health are all considered as part of the complex nexus of interactions that exist between the experience of homelessness and health outcomes. While intersectional approaches might have been obscured (Kapilashrami *et al.*, 2015), public health approaches have been hugely successful in providing the robust evidence to assert that a social gradient in health exists and for arguing that resources should be focused on prevention and the early years in life. In this chapter, the health of 'hidden' homeless groups is explored, including women, young people and people who identify as lesbian, gay, bisexual, and transgender (LGBT). These debates interrogate the ways that gender (Baptista, 2010), racism and stigma (Reimer-Kirkham and Sharma, 2011) all intersect in marginal lives to shape health and well-being (Bauer, 2014; Bowleg, 2012; Hankivsky, 2012).

Chapter 7 takes a different approach, where ACEs, psychologically informed environments (PIE) and trauma-informed approaches to care are discussed 'in conversation' with consultant clinical psychologist Dr Adam Burley. Drawing on many years of working with people who experience social exclusion and homelessness, Dr Burley discusses his experience of working with people who experience profound trauma in their lives and the importance of relationships to healthy functioning. This chapter is concluded with a 'case study' of lived experience of one of the people he has worked with, and it emphasises the importance of trauma-informed approaches to care.

ER 2

Contemporary Urban Marginality: Health inequalities in a globalising world

This chapter will draw on socio-political theory to explore the ways that globalisation has created urban centres of health inequity and will foreground global structural causes of homelessness. It will explore how the process of entering and exiting homelessness at a local level is affected by the interaction of global economic, demographic and idealised (neoliberal) forces and relate this to healthcare policy and practice.

Globalisation and health

Globalisation – 'the increased economic, political, and social interconnectedness of the world' (Giddens, 2018) – has created extraordinary advances in human health, wealth and well-being over the last five decades. In 2017, president of the World Bank, Jim Yong Kim, told the annual meeting of the World Bank and International Monetary Fund that China has seen unprecedented economic growth since the start of the economic reforms, lifting 800 billion people out of poverty, which he called 'a great story in human history' (Business Standard, 2017). India is the largest democracy in the world, has a rapidly growing middle class and boasts the largest film industry in the world, with an estimated value of US$101 million (Statista, 2017). The global economic forecast is set to continue for a 3.9% increase in economic growth in 2019 (World Bank, 2018a), and since 1990 alone the number of people living on less than US$1.90 a day – the international measure of extreme poverty – has fallen by more than a half (UNDP, 2015).

In terms of health and well-being, there have been undoubted gains. Since 1990, the world has seen a 50% decrease in annual child deaths since 1990, which have now dropped to below 6 million for the first time (WHO, 2017). The average child born in 1950 could expect to live to just forty-eight years old; today, that child could expect to live to seventy-two years (WHO, 2016a). The number of people who are dying from HIV and malaria has been halved since the millennium development goals (MDGs) were set (UN, 2000), and life expectancy has increased in almost every country of the globe (WHO, 2017). More than two billion people now have access to safe drinking water and good sanitation for the first time (UNDP, 2015). Margaret Chan, director general of the World Health Organization (WHO) 2007–17, asserts that 'in a world facing considerable uncertainty, international health development is a unifying – and uplifting – force for the good of humanity' (WHO, 2017, p. 2).

It is clear that, while the march of global capitalism has created undoubted wealth in many previously low-income countries, the gains have not been evenly distributed through society. Inequalities both within and between countries have never been as great, and global wealth is increasingly being collected in the hands of the few. India now boasts a gross domestic product (GDP) of US$2.5 trillion (World Bank, 2018b), a burgeoning middle class and a space programme, but 270 million people remain in absolute poverty (World Bank, 2016). As geo-political tensions increase between Russia and the USA, India and China compete to be the global economic powerhouses of the future. Nonetheless, the winners and losers of global capitalism are located in different worlds: those who jet around the globe in pursuit of designer goods, luxury properties and Michelin-starred meals; those who live next to open sewers to dig in rubbish dumps for a daily meal. While there has always been poverty, recent unprecedented economic growth has raised concerns that the gap between those who have and those who have not is not only becoming wider, but it is also creating discontented and sick societies (Pickett and Wilkinson, 2010). Despite being the largest global economy, the USA has the third highest rates of poverty of any country in the world at 16.9% (OECD, 2017). In fact, Robert Shiller, Nobel Prize winner in Economics in 2013, stated 'the most important problem we are facing now, today ... is rising inequality' (cited by Dorling, 2014).

Scholars have been challenging the unbridled success thesis of global capitalism for the last two decades and highlighting the 'shadow side' of capitalism and global consumption – namely the rise of global inequalities. The work of leading thinker and geographer Professor Danny Dorling has been influential in expanding this work: in the first chapter of his book *Inequality and the 1%*, he starts by asking the question: 'Can we afford the superrich?' He then goes on to unpack the many ways that inequality is destroying our childhood, working environment, wealth and health (Dorling, 2014). This is seen in recent evidence that highlights the pay gap between the average worker and senior management in many of the world's multinational companies. Research from Oxfam in 2015 asserted that the richest 1% of the world owned more wealth than the rest of the world (Oxfam, 2015). In 2017, it published a second report, 'An economy for the 99%', showing that eight billionaires now own the same wealth as the 3.6 billion people who are the poorest part of the world (Oxfam, 2017). Concern is not only being raised by scholars and NGOs: in a recent report, the Organisation for Economic Cooperation and Development (OECD) warned:

> The long-run increase in income inequality not only raises social and political concerns, but also economic ones. It tends to drag down GDP growth, due to the rising distance of the lower 40% from the rest of society. Lower income people have been prevented from realising their human capital potential, which is bad for the economy as a whole (OECD, 2015, no page numbers).

As scholars in the field of economics and politics are increasingly turning their attention to the consequences of growing economic inequity in our world and offering alternative models for economic, environmental and human development (Raworth, 2017), epidemiologists and public health researchers have turned their attention to highlight the links between economic inequality and health inequality. These health inequalities exist between and within societies. Noncommunicable diseases (NCDs), such as diabetes, cardiovascular diseases (for example, stroke and heart attacks), cancers, chronic obstructive pulmonary disease and asthma, account for the leading causes of death globally (WHO, 2018b), responsible for 41 million deaths each year, which is 71% of all deaths. Contrary to popular belief that these diseases are the so-called diseases of affluence, the burden of NCDs is actually located in middle-income and, increasingly, low-income countries (WHO, 2018a). A social gradient of health exists, and the lower people are in the social hierarchy the higher their risk of NCDs. Health cannot be improved without dealing with the social determinants of health, the 'causes of the causes' (Marmot, 2017a, p. 24), which are:

> the conditions in which people are born, grow, live, work and age. These circumstances are shaped by the distribution of money, power and resources at global, national and local levels (WHO, 2008, p. 4).

People who live as homeless are no different to the rest of the global population: positioned within the social gradient of health – albeit at the most extreme end – they are exposed to the rise of NCDs, and increasingly healthcare practitioners and researchers are drawing attention to the healthcare issues as experienced by an ageing homeless population (Sermons and Henry, 2010; Cohen, 2012). Crane and Joly (2014) carried out a review of older homeless people across nine high-income countries including Australia, USA, Canada and Japan and found that there is a growing number of older people experiencing homelessness. This is a result of two main factors: people who have been homeless for some time are growing older; and some people are entering homelessness for the first time in older age, largely because of bereavement or problems with housing tenure. The authors point out that there are increasing numbers of people who are homeless over the age of sixty-five years and that many older people who experience homelessness have chronic health needs that are similar to people much older than them in age. Brown *et al.* (2010) assert that services need to be designed to meet the needs of older homeless people, recognising changing demographics. Fazel *et al.* (2014) note an increased mortality and morbidity for people living with homelessness because of cardiovascular disease. Baggett *et al.* (2013), likewise, found that older homeless people in Boston, USA died from cardiovascular diseases and cancer – like the general population – but 10–15 years earlier. Age-related cognitive impairment and increased functional decline have also been noted with older people who identify as homeless (Brown *et al.*, 2012; Lebrun-Harris *et al.*, 2010). In Brown *et al.'s* (2013) study of older people experiencing homelessness in shelters in the USA, 40% demonstrated cognitive impairment and 59% traumatic brain injury. In addition, older people who are homeless are less likely to have contact with healthcare staff (Hwang *et al.*, 2008) and, increasingly, access to specialist services such as hospice and end-of-life care is problematic (McNeil *et al.*, 2012). In Ottawa, Canada, a coalition of community leaders developed Canada's first emergency-based, shelter-based hospice, and this now operates a sixteen-bed palliative care programme integrated into an emergency shelter in downtown Ottawa (Guirguis-Younger and McNeil, 2014). As the global population ages and is impacted by the rise in NCDs, so too is the 'homeless population'.

Health inequalities as a consequence of global inequalities

Health inequalities are increasingly recognised by the international health community as unjust; the WHO states: 'the social determinants of health are mostly responsible for health inequities – the unfair and avoidable difference in health status seen within and between countries' (WHO, 2018a, no page). Health inequalities between countries have been evident for many years and, despite global success in improving life expectancy and child mortality, inequalities between and within countries remain. Worldwide, life expectancy has been growing in most countries since the Second World War: in 1990, average life expectancy at birth was sixty-four years; in 2015, it was 71.4 years and more than seventy years in eighty-two countries (UN, 2017). Nonetheless, looking at child – under-five – mortality rates, it is clear that success has been very uneven. Since the MDGs were set in 2000 to reduce child mortality by two-thirds, only the European region has reached this, with the Africa region achieving a reduction in child mortality by only 53% (UN, 2017). In addition, in the Africa region, life expectancy at birth increased by 9.7 years, whereas it was only eight years in the Asia region. Significantly, these two continents also had the biggest population growth during this period: in Africa, the population grew from 635 million to 1.2 billion; and in Asia from 3.2 billion to 4.4 billion (UN, 2017). In 2015, the global health community through the United Nations (UN) set the 2030 Agenda for Sustainable Development, which identified seventeen new targets, called sustainable development goals (SDGs) (UN, 2016). These goals place the emphasis on equity, access to primary healthcare and the links between health and the social determinants of health and environmental degradation, rather than on the narrow focus of disease in the MDGs (WHO, 2016b).

While the UK has been recognised as progressive in policy efforts to reduce health inequalities between 1997 and 2010, the gap between the health outcomes of the richest and the poorest in society continues to widen (Bambra, 2012; Mackenbach, 2011). The UK have been described 'historically and internationally unique' in its efforts to tackle health inequalities (Mackenbach, 2011, p. 1249), yet homelessness continues to rise. In an increasingly politicised approach to public health and health inequalities, researchers assert that the consequences of neoliberalism is that it makes us ill (Schrecker and Bambra, 2015). Since *The Black Report* (Department of Health and Social Security, 1980) first uncovered the extent to which ill health and death were unequally distributed across the population of Britain, a plethora of research-based evidence has testified to the multiple ways that health is influenced by the wider social determinants of health and poverty. Equity is a strong driver of health policy in Scotland as research increasingly highlights the detrimental impact on health that the 'gap' itself is having (Marmot, 2015a). *The Spirit Level* (Pickett and Wilkinson, 2010) exposed the multiple ways that inequity in society impacts negatively on the health and well-being of Western societies – the greater the inequity 'gap', the greater the incidences of crime, mental ill health etc. In their most recent book, *The Inner Level*, the authors present a compelling case of the ways that more equal societies reduce stress and improve mental health and well-being (Wilkinson and Pickett, 2018).

It is within this global context of economic and health inequalities that homelessness can be understood within global urban areas as post-deindustrialised nation states are shaped by a capitalist service economy. At a UK national level, people in the north are consistently found to suffer more ill health than those in the south (Whitehead and Doran, 2011). Public Health England reports data that shows people in Manchester were more than twice as likely to die early than people in the south of England in Wokingham (Public Health England, 2016), and researchers suggest that these health divides are explained by the social and economic inequality between these two areas (Doran and Whitehead, 2004; Copeland *et al.,* 2015). The English regions have been unevenly impacted by deindustrialisation, with the northern regions experiencing higher levels of unemployment and related ill health (Kontopantelis *et al.,* 2018). Unemployment has been found to be a key social risk factor for increased mortality and ill health (Bambra, 2011), as is homelessness.

The national and local picture in the UK is not unique: researchers have travelled between different neighbourhoods in several different cities and found that the gap between the life expectancy within these cities is marked. In Baltimore, USA, there is a twenty-year difference in life expectancy between males in the inner-city Upton area and the affluent Greater Roland Park (Marmot, 2015b), and in Stockton-on-Tees in the north-east of England, which has the highest geographical health inequalities in England, there is a life expectancy at birth gap of seventeen years for males and eleven years for women (Bhandari et al., 2017).

Urbanisation, housing and employment: Implications for health

It is clear that, while globalisation has increased wealth and health, it has done so in an uneven way (Peck and Tickell, 2002). Inequity of the fruits of globalisation has not only been felt between the rich and the poor, but also between the rural and the urban economies. As the global population grows, globalisation is creating global urbanisation, where migration shapes new urban landscapes. As young people flock to the cities in search of employment and wealth, rural areas stagnate and decay. The result of this rapid urbanisation is increasingly crowded cities, where people live in overcrowded accommodation, and slum areas on the edges of cities proliferate. Global megacities have been created at the expense of good housing, sustainable income and adequate health and educational opportunities. In low-income countries, the trend is towards urbanisation; young people leave the villages and migrate towards the cities in search of employment and wealth. While the newspapers feed the dream, many people exist in the urban slums, scraping together a living in low-paid, insecure and dangerous jobs. It is currently estimated that 828 million people live in slums, representing one-third of the urban population globally (WHO, 2018b). The health outcomes for people who live in overcrowded and inadequate housing is poor due to stagnant water, overcrowding, open sewage, toxic dump sites and inadequate shelter (WHO, 2018b). Pickett and Pearl (2001) also remind us of the less tangible community features such as high unemployment rates, stress, crime, violence, political empowerment and civic engagement that also impact on health in both positive and negative ways.

As the megacities of the Global South spawn slum areas and burgeoning shanty towns, the rise of the uber-wealthy and global elite has created a housing crisis in the world's most affluent cities: London, New York, Paris,

Sydney and Vancouver. Global cities have become hubs of transnational networks (Sassen, 2011; 2012) dominated by the need to attract capital investment at the expense of housing the local population. The result is precarious labour markets and the commodification of the housing market. As prime properties are bought up by the global elite, ordinary people – particularly the youth – struggle to survive in the housing market, paying up to 80% of average incomes on housing rents and are forced to move to the outskirts of the cities for affordable housing (Dillabough and Kennelly, 2010). The 2008 financial crisis resulted in the marketisation of social housing (Kennett *et al.*, 2013) and the privatisation of social housing stocks. Worldwide, many countries have faced large-scale social challenges: high levels of unemployment and social exclusion. The era of austerity has been directly observable in many countries, also in the social, political and cultural determinants of population health (Stuckler and Basu, 2013). There is a growing understanding of the fact that economic cycles, structures and societal conditions necessarily reflect well-being and related inequalities over a long period of time. The UK is in a housing crisis as experts predict that 300,000 houses need to be built over the next decade to accommodate the expanding population.

In the UK, neoliberal ideology has opened up the house building market to unbridled expansion for profit, at the expense of affordable and social housing. Welfare state settlements in the USA, UK and Australia following the Second World War did not create the wealth-for-all that was promised following peace, but a crisis in housing in the late 1970s and 80s and recreated poverty in the form of homelessness on the streets. Driven by Conservative political values under Margaret Thatcher in the 1980s, social housing was sold off to tenants at radically reduced rates, and as a consequence social housing stock in many of our cities is woefully inadequate. As neoliberal values reward a global elite, the downward pressure on the average worker begins to be felt as substandard and crowded housing, high rents and precarious lives. While poverty is nothing new, social groupings are being reordered in a global economy where a new precariat has emerged. Standing (2011) has reconceptualised global social groupings in our contemporary world, identifying the precariat as a new social grouping, defined by unstable employment contracts and zero-hours contracts, high student debt, high mobility and low employment security. The precariat then becomes very vulnerable to changes in the global market and local economy. Unless the 'bank of mum and dad' can bale young people out of poverty, they enter an unstable and precarious existence.

As homelessness emerged as an issue to be 'fixed' in the 1980s in many cities in the UK, Australia, Europe and USA, governmentality theorists described the shift from welfare liberal to neoliberal modes of governance (Rose, 1991; 1999). Under these neoliberal models, citizens were reimagined as individual consumers with obligations to the state to work and contribute to economic success. The success, or failure, of the citizen was no longer given according to their ability to support themselves through universal welfare support, but by their capacity to engage with the flexible economy. Within this approach, global capitalism expects global citizens, and for these citizens to be active in achieving the rewards of capital growth. Capitalism is defined as 'a system of generalised commodity production in which wealth is owned privately and economic life is organised according to market principles' (Heywood, 2011, p. 84). The prevailing view among economists is that neoliberalism is the only way to achieve global prosperity, where 'free market forces, achieved by minimizing governmental restrictions on business, provide the only route to economic growth. Neoliberalism holds that global free trade will enable all countries to prosper' (Giddens, 2018). The underlying premise is that this will only be possible if individuals work to contribute to the economic growth and that governmental regulation is eliminated.

The idea of the 'active' or 'passive' citizen is a strong narrative thread running through these ideas: to be a citizen is to be employed, actively working and contributing to society; to be 'passive' and the recipient of help is to be positioned as morally in need of 'redemption' and of 'turning around'. Arnold (2004) argues that, in leaving behind the family and village bonds of feudal societies, individuals now interact directly with the state through neoliberal structures and need to find validity and recognition from the state. To be a 'real' valid person, individuals are required to be productive as the 'active citizen'. People who are homeless, particularly harmful substance users or those who are cognitively impaired, are positioned in society as in need of protection - 'passive citizen' at best, or a burden on society at worst. In addition, in a globalised world, an increasing number of homeless migrants are exploited and left to negotiate street life as a non-citizen (Waite *et al.*, 2015). By linking personal validity so much to citizenship, both political and social, individual interactions with the state and personal legacy, identity and potential are bound up in the 'liminal space' between passive and active citizenship (Arnold, 2004).

In the everyday, the notion of 'skivers' and 'strivers' has popularised the idea that people are either pushing on in society to earn their own way or are letting others do it for them. This intensification of moral judgement on the people who are the most disadvantaged in society has been highlighted by several scholars in the UK and North America (Valentine and Harris, 2014; Upton, 2016), while others have argued that the vilification of the unemployed is nothing new (Monbiot, 2015) and has been present over the last 200 years. The UK press debate this within the context of recent welfare reforms (Williams, 2013) as homelessness continues to grow in the high-income economies of Europe, North America and Australia. Sociologist and international scholar Zygmunt Bauman (2013) argues that modernity has created a world of 'wasted lives', where the losers of globalisation are caught in precarious lives and are washed to the bottom of society. Refugees, asylum seekers and undocumented migrants are often positioned even lower than the local citizen who experiences homelessness. In addition, Snow and Mulcahy (2001) argue that the gentrification of urban spaces has resulted in new forms of governance and social control in cities. Areas that were once public space for the homeless have become private space, and the homeless have become squeezed out into new urban spaces (Rankin et al., 2015; Zukin et al., 2015). As an example, DeVerteuil (2006) argues that modern architecture in Los Angeles is actively used to obscure homeless shelters. Contributing to these debates, Tyler (2013) asserts that refugees and people seeking asylum are positioned as 'revolting subjects' in a neoliberal age – social problems to be solved. Without social, political or identity representation, they occupy a new political space in a globalising world (Fraser, 2008).

New political spaces: Migration, health and homelessness

Globalisation has not only created a world where the global flow of goods and services has taken on a new velocity and intensity, but so too has the global flow of people. Into this urbanising, unstable and precarious global landscape, people move around the world in new and unprecedented ways. While countries increasingly control their borders, migrants arrive as students, workers and refugees. Entering global cities, they jostle for jobs, for recognition, for housing and for security. In the churn of these contemporary global cities, people fall through the cracks in housing availability, social welfare provision and healthcare accessibility. Homelessness emerges from these cracks; many people are unable to find affordable housing; standardised tenancies do not meet individual needs; people are unable to negotiate a global landscape of citizenship and identity in a new land, unable to meet the costs of living in a global megacity. In addition, the forces of global migration bring the displaced, the disadvantaged and the destitute to the city streets. And this trend appears to be set for the foreseeable future. Paul Collier argues that the global income gap will continue to grow as global capitalism expands to forge a 'grotesquely wide' (Collier, 2013, p. 50) income gap between rich and poor and migration progresses to accelerate. The result, he argues, is that 'for the foreseeable future, international migration will not reach equilibrium: we have been observing the beginnings of disequilibrium of epic proportions' (Collier, 2013, p. 51).

While rapid urbanisation and increasing pressure in the city is one cause of homelessness, conflict and global instability are clearly others. While we may individually wash our hands of responsibility for these shifting groups of humanity, Bauman (2017, p. 5) lays the blame squarely on the:

> collateral damage done by the fatally misjudged, ill-starred and calamitous military expeditions to Afghanistan and Iraq, which ended in the replacing of dictatorial regimes by the open-all-hours theatre of unruliness and the frenzy of violence – aided and abetted by the global arms trade unleashed from control and beefed up by the profit-greedy arms industry, with the tacit (though all too often proudly displayed in public at international arms fairs) support of GNP-rise-greedy governments (Bauman, 2017, p. 5).

Conclusion

In this chapter, homelessness in the local domain is framed as a consequence of global pressures. While it is acknowledged that global capitalism has brought unprecedented wealth and health, it has done so in an uneven way, and those who experience homelessness are the consequence of global inequalities. Health inequalities can be mapped as a social gradient, where those who live with the greatest poverty are also exposed to the worst health outcomes. Homelessness in this context becomes a symptom experience social exclusion and homelessness, Dr Burley discusses his experience of working with people who experience profound trauma in their lives and the importance of relationships to healthy functioning. This chapter is concluded with a 'case study' of lived experience of one of the people he has worked with, and it emphasises the importance of trauma-informed approaches to care.

CHAPTER 2

Contemporary Urban Marginality: Health inequalities in a globalising world

This chapter will draw on socio-political theory to explore the ways that globalisation has created urban centres of health inequity and will foreground global structural causes of homelessness. It will explore how the process of entering and exiting homelessness at a local level is affected by the interaction of global economic, demographic and idealised (neoliberal) forces and relate this to healthcare policy and practice.

Globalisation and health

Globalisation – 'the increased economic, political, and social interconnectedness of the world' (Giddens, 2018) – has created extraordinary advances in human health, wealth and well-being over the last five decades. In 2017, president of the World Bank, Jim Yong Kim, told the annual meeting of the World Bank and International Monetary Fund that China has seen unprecedented economic growth since the start of the economic reforms, lifting 800 billion people out of poverty, which he called 'a great story in human history' (Business Standard, 2017). India is the largest democracy in the world, has a rapidly growing middle class and boasts the largest film industry in the world, with an estimated value of US$101 million (Statista, 2017). The global economic forecast is set to continue for a 3.9% increase in economic growth in 2019 (World Bank, 2018a), and since 1990 alone the number of people living on less than US$1.90 a day – the international measure of extreme poverty – has fallen by more than a half (UNDP, 2015).

In terms of health and well-being, there have been undoubted gains. Since 1990, the world has seen a 50% decrease in annual child deaths agreement the EU has made with Turkey to keep asylum seekers from crossing the Aegean sea to Greece. As walls are erected against what the artist Ai Weiwei's recent documentary terms the 'Human flow' (Amazon Studios, 2017), political campaigns debate dissatisfaction with European open borders, as in the Brexit referendum in June 2016 in the UK, and centre around those migrants – largely African – who are no longer welcome in Italy, as evidenced in their March 2018 election.

The last decade has not only seen an increase in absolute numbers of people who are now experiencing forced migration but also a change from single – usually male – migration to the movement of whole families. Women and children now constitute the majority of refugees globally, and the resettlement of forced migrants has become focused on urban centres rather than in refugee camps (Betts and Collier, 2017; UNHCR, 2018). As patterns of movement and the composition of forced migration changes, the traditional agencies set up following the Second World War to 'manage' forced migration, primarily the United Nations High Commission for Refugees (UNHCR), struggle to cope with the new opportunities that globalisation both offers and denies forced migrants, as people seek new ways of living, surviving and being.

The UNHCR documented 68.5 million forcibly displaced people worldwide in 2017 – the highest number ever in recorded history. Some 25.4 million of these are refugees, and 50% are under the age of eighteen years. The majority of refugees worldwide (57%) come from three countries: South Sudan (2.4 million); Afghanistan (2.6 million) and Syria (6.5 million). While low- and middle-income countries continue to accept the vast majority of the world's global refugees, the protracted war in Syria has seen an increasing number of people crossing the Mediterranean sea to reach Europe, primarily through Italy and Greece. Lebanon, Turkey, Uganda and Pakistan continue to accept the largest numbers of refugees globally, taking 1.0 million, 3.5 million, 1.4 million and 1.4 million respectively (UNHCR, 2018). Nonetheless, the newspaper headlines in Europe proclaim a 'flood' of refugees into Italy and Greece since 2015. In reality, only 25% of the world's refugees make it to European shores, but 2015 witnessed a change in global geopolitics, and as a consequence the mass migration of people from Syria and north Africa to initially the tiny Italian island of Lampedusa and, more recently, to the Greek island of Lesbos.

In their powerful book *Refuge: Transforming a Broken Refugee System,*
Betts and Collier (2017) describe the moment in 2015 when a young Tuni-
sian man, Mohamed Bouazizi, set fire to himself on 17 December 2010,
and died of his burns. This moment, they argue, triggered the 'Arab Spring'
and 'became the equivalent of the bullet fired by the assassin Gavrilo Prin-
cip which killed Archduke Franz Ferdinand and triggered the First World
War' (Collier and Betts, 2017, p. 67). While the so-called Arab Spring was
initially seen as a cause for rejoicing and celebration of a new-found freedom from tyrannical regimes, it soon turned into the reality of the disin-
tegration of governance in Libya, Syria and Tunisia. The consequence of a
breakdown in tyrannical regimes opened the way for warlords to reassert
their rule in Libya and for mass protests in Tunisia. As the rule of law disintegrated in the countries of north Africa bordering the Mediterranean sea,
and calls for democracy rapidly disintegrated into violence and conflict,
it did not take long for the people traffickers to seize their opportunity
and to develop routes across the hazardous Mediterranean to Lampedusa.
Flimsy boats set sail across the Mediterranean sea carrying young men
and families seeking safety on European shores, but many did not make it:
7,000 people died in only one month – April – in 2015 alone. In response
to this humanitarian crisis, the ship *Aquarius Aquarium* was chartered by
the NGO SOS Méditerranée. Rescuing people in overcrowded dinghies
only a few hundred metres from the north African shore, the *Aquarius
Aquarium* inadvertently became an aid to the people traffickers; they were
saving people from drowning in the hazardous waters, while providing a
'taxi' service to Italian shores for the fleeing migrants. The rest of Europe
looked on; refusing to take responsibility for the horrors unfolding on Italian shores, European leaders upheld the Dublin Regulation and asserted
that newly arrived migrants were registered in the first country of arrival.

Unlike the refugees arriving in Turkey, who were settled by the UNHCR
in refugee camps, the migrants arriving in Italy, and subsequently Greece,
passed through the countries heading north. The Italian government,
overwhelmed by the numbers of migrants arriving on their shores and
frustrated by the lack of action by other EU states, allowed migrants to be
registered and then to move north. As Hungary, Austria and the Czech
Republic closed their borders using armed police and razor wire, Chancel-
lor Angela Merkel of Germany declared in 2015 that her country would
accept 1 million migrants. Refugees poured into Germany until her bor-

ders closed in 2016. Meanwhile, the UNHCR looked on, largely powerless to either force action by European governments, nor able to manage the crisis that was unfolding before their very eyes. Betts and Collier (2017, p. 61) assert: 'to date, the predominant political response to the Syrian refugee crisis has not been a rethink of policy: it has been panic. Prepare for headless chickens.' The international agency that had been set up in 1945 to manage the resettlement of the Jews following the Second World War was shown to be inadequate to manage or support the movement of people in the new globalised era. While many called for a root-and-branch reform of the UNHCR (Betts and Collier, 2017), migrants used new global connectedness to track opportunities and family members in other parts of Europe and to move where conditions were conducive to finding citizenship and a work permit.

The dangers to health, and life, of refugees were starkly exemplified on the day a photograph shocked the world as the body of the toddler Alan Kurdi was scooped off the sands of Bodrum. Into the churn of moving – and dying – people, government agencies and NGOs have struggled to meet the health and well-being needs of people transitioning from war, conflict and violence through changing borders and political walls.

Forced migrants experience multiple forms of simultaneous homelessness: not only losing the safety and security of a physical place to live but also being displaced from the wider family, community and the cultural and social norms of what it means to be home. They often face hostility, racial hatred and isolation in host countries, which impact negatively on mental health and well-being. In research undertaken by Phillimore *et al.* (2007) in the UK, community refugee researchers found that racism and the stigmatisation of asylum seekers by the state also contributed to mental ill health.

While many people seeking asylum and refugees are given shelter, housing is only a physical location and is a long road from finding a home. While home is a psychological concept associated with personal and social meanings embedded in physical space (Coolen and Meesters, 2012), it is also inextricably linked to culture (Magat, 1999; Rapoport, 2000), and journeys 'away from home' are important because, in its absence, individuals are forced to reflect on its meaning, belonging and identity (Case, 1996). As people move through different countries and navigate the challenges of each country, encountering various forms of displacement and homelessness, people experience trauma, develop resilience and negotiate life to meet their needs within the resources available to them at that time and in that country. Against a discourse of migration as an 'invasive process' (Hall, 2015b, p. 854), the politics of migration continue to escalate (Gilroy, 2004; Hall, 2015a), and frequently migrants are met with hostility and aggression in the receiving countries. As I write, news agencies report that racial hatred for Venezuelan refugees is bubbling over in Peru (Sanchez, 2018). The health needs of refugees and people seeking asylum are multifaceted and are shaped by each stage of the refugee 'journey'.

Health and well-being: The experience of forced migrants
The reality for many people who are forcibly displaced is that their first experience of the dream of safety is the reality of overcrowded reception centres, under-resourced refugee camps in low-income countries or fragile shelter in the urban centres of the world. The causes of forced migration – war, conflict and natural disaster – are unpredictable, and organisations are often reactive, rather than proactive, in response (Bradby et al., 2015). Refugee camps can be dangerous places where overcrowding gives rise to outbreaks of infectious disease, and violence within the camps is evident. For north African and Syrian migrants arriving in Europe across the Aegean sea in 2015, makeshift reception centres were often in derelict old factories, tented camps or abandoned holiday villages. Overcrowding and poor sanitation exposed people to vermin and disease, and food was often at minimum levels; into this context, healthcare needs were met on an emergency rather than a planned basis (Oxford Analytica, 2016). Increasingly, refugees encounter long delays in refugee reception centres (Blitz et al., 2017) and resettlement processes to a safe haven are protracted and stressful.

In general, on arrival in a safe country, a range of diverse systems operate to meet the health needs of forced migrants, focusing on a wide range of health issues. EU public health experts assert that migrants are often healthy when they arrive in a country of safety and do not pose a significant health threat (Semenza et al., 2016). Nonetheless, migrants are at risk of infection due to overcrowding and precarious access to healthcare services, so many countries screen for infectious disease on entry to the country (Einterz et al., 2018). In the USA, the focus is primarily on communicable diseases, where the Centers for Disease Control and Prevention (CDC) recommends screening all refugees for sexually transmitted infections, such as HIV, and blood tests for other diseases such as schistosomiasis. In the majority of high-income countries, people seeking asylum and refugees are screened for infectious diseases – and increasingly for NCDs. While a range of different screening processes and tools are used to assess the health of forced migrants on arrival in a safe country, most countries focus on infectious diseases (including HIV, tuberculosis, hepatitis A, B and C and sexually transmitted infections), immunisations, pregnancy, parasites in the gut and mental health screening (Einterz *et al.*, 2018). Increasingly, women are also being offered cervical cancer screening (Percac-Lima *et al.*, 2013).

The European Parliament and Council (directive 2013/33/EU) recognises that people seeking asylum and refugees have additional health needs to the local population, including support following violence, rape, torture and human rights violations, and it states that individual countries should assess the health needs of this group as soon as possible within a reasonable time period. Nonetheless, the literature highlights multiple difficulties that people seeking asylum and refugees have in accessing healthcare and preventative services in Australia (Drummond *et al.*, 2011), the EU (Rosano, 2018) and North America (Caulford and Vali, 2006).

The health needs of people seeking asylum and refugees have been well documented across a range of different countries and contexts, and while scholars assert that there is high heterogeneity across countries and studies, and subsequent comparison of data proves very difficult (Bradby *et al.*, 2015), research has consistently identified particular health issues with this population (Abubakar *et al.*, 2016). Comparative studies between refugee and non-refugee groups in high-income countries have found that refugees suffer poorer health outcomes than other migrants (Hollander, 2013). Mental health issues are overrepresented in refugee populations as compared to non-refugee groups (Georgiadou *et al.*, 2017), particularly post-traumatic stress disorder (PTSD), depression and anxiety disorders, with a prevalence rate of 30% (Alpak *et al.*, 2015). This is not surprising, given that many forced migrants experience trauma (Bith-Melander *et al.*, 2017) as they flee persecution, violence and war (Shannon *et al.*, 2015; UNHCR, 2018. Many people have experienced torture (Pettitt, 2013). Some scholars have termed the magnitude of this trauma a 'mental health crisis'

(Anagnostopoulos *et al.*, 2016), while others focus on the resilience of people who seek asylum (Sen, 2016) and argue that forced migrants have a health advantage when they enter a country of refuge and that health only disintegrates as time goes on living in a host country.

Stigmatisation, language barriers, poor health literacy and concerns about confidentiality have all been shown to contribute to the low use of primary care services and high use of accident and emergency services by migrants. Screening for infectious diseases such as HIV and TB can be stigmatising, and Fassil (2000) argues that screening is more to do with protecting the host population rather than benefiting the health of newly arrived refugees. Racism and discrimination have also been shown to impact negatively on the health of refugees and people seeking asylum (Kastrup, 2016). Although research has repeatedly demonstrated that screening for mental ill health and receiving appropriate treatment can reduce hospital attendance and improve health outcomes for torture survivors (Song *et al.*, 2018), refugees with PTSD and depression find that access is frequently hindered by political debates around access to and use of public services, populism and national security concerns.

Health needs of unaccompanied minors and adolescents

Unaccompanied minors and adolescents have been shown to be at particular risk of violence, death and poor mental health (Montgomery, 2011), and there is wide concern around the high levels of unmet mental health issues with refugee children and unaccompanied minors (Bean *et al.*, 2007). Unaccompanied minors are often not distinguished from adult refugees, and their needs are ignored (Derluyn and Broekaert, 2008). Youth mental health – anxiety, depression and aggression – is an important health issue in refugee camps, but a recent systematic review by Vossoughi *et al.* (2016) noted that different definitions and measures across different countries made comparison difficult. Refugee and internally displaced people are a highly diverse group. Nonetheless, most studies focus on the relationship between unaccompanied minors in high-income countries and exposure to violence at an early stage of child development. This is understood to be an important risk factor for physical, psychological and socio-developmental health (Reed *et al.*, 2012). Protective factors in a safe country include local community support and strong friendships, participation in school and language proficiency (Montgomery, 2011).

The flight from 'home' to a safe country is in itself fraught with danger. Newspaper reports regularly run stories of young people killed in Calais while trying to get to the UK: Raheemullah Oryakhel, fourteen years, was hit by a car in 2016 (BBC, 2016); and Abdullah Dilsouz, fifteen years, was run over by a truck in 2017 (Guardian, 2018). Despite well-established child safeguarding legislation in Europe (UNICEF, 1989), it is estimated that 10,000 refugee children go missing in Europe each year (European Parliament, 2016). A report by the National Society for the Prevention of Cruelty to Children (Jamieson, 2018) raised concern that 128 children were missing from the refugee camps in Calais and were at risk of physical and sexual abuse and child trafficking.

Health needs of women migrants: Pregnancy, maternal health and sexual abuse

Scholars have also highlighted the gendered sources of distress and resilience among refugees (Casey et al., 2008; Stempel et al., 2016), where it is increasingly recognised that women experience particular healthcare needs in relation to pregnancy, maternal health and sexual health. Women are especially vulnerable to sexual abuse, rape and physical assault, and scholars in the past have raised concern that their vulnerabilities have not been taken seriously (Wallace, 1990).

In recent years, there has been more focus on the health needs of refugee and displaced women and children, particularly in relation to the use of rape as a tool of war. Women and children are particularly at risk from gender-based violence as they flee their own country, from warlords, armed gangs and border guards, but the arrival at a refugee camp is not necessarily a 'safe haven'. Refugee camps have been shown to be very dangerous places for poor and displaced women and children, where they are vulnerable to sexual exploitation from men within the camps as they search for firewood and food. As traditional gender roles and responsibilities are reshaped in the refugee camps, displaced women use sex work as a means of survival. While the sexual exploitation of women and children in refugee camps by humanitarian aid workers has been news headlines in many countries, this is not new (Ferris, 2007). UNHCR and Save the Children UK carried out research in 2002 on the sexual violence and exploitation of children in Liberia, Guinea and Sierra Leone (UNHCR and Save the Children UK, 2002) and found that abuse of children aged 13–18 years by NGO workers was widespread. Without any power to negotiate and in a very vulnerable position because of poverty and displacement, sexual abuse by NGO workers is easily covered over. As one participant in the UNHCR and Save the Children study (2002, p. 44) explained:

> If I tell you the name of the NGO worker I have to have sex with, he will get fired, and then how will I feed my child and myself? (Girl-mother, Guinea)

During settlement in a 'safe haven' country, refugee women have been found to be at particular risk when living in intimate relationships where coercive control or violence is present, as they have little family support, have difficulties in navigating the health and social care system and are constrained by cultural expectations around marriage (Ahmad *et al.* 2009; Crawley *et al.*, 2011). Nonetheless, the literature lacks differentiation and, as the majority of studies are across a very wide range of different nationalities and reasons for migration, comparison is difficult. In a systematic review of the literature on immigrant women's experiences of family violence, Australian researchers found notably few studies that specifically examined the prevalence of family violence against refugee and displaced women (Vaughan *et al.*, 2015). The literature suggests that refugee and displaced women's experiences of family violence is wide and nuanced. In research by Rees and Pease (2007), in a qualitative study across a diverse range of refugee women in Melbourne, Australia, it was found that family violence was understood as both physical violence and controlling behaviour (financial and social control).

Cultural understandings of family violence vary widely between different cultures and countries: west African women in Australia recognised only physical violence but not controlling behaviours that might be understood within the Australian context, such as coercive control. Other cultures have been found to be unfamiliar with rape in marriage, and this has limited reporting and interventions (Ahmad *et al.*, 2009). When in the host country, safety is not guaranteed as many undocumented migrant women are particularly vulnerable to sexual abuse and violence as they are told that their eligibility to stay in the country depends on whether they stay as dependents with a partner (Geddie, 2009). Support organisations present many case studies of women who have felt that they have had to stay in abusive relationships because they feared that their immigration status would be impacted if they left the relationship (Maternity Action, 2018; Safety4Sisters, 2016). Crawley *et al.* (2011) describe the lives of women who become homeless following the asylum process in the UK as entering into transactional or exploitative relationships in order to survive. They documented: 'destitute asylum seekers providing childcare, cooking and/or housework … and sometimes even sex in exchange for meals, small amounts of cash, shelter, or other daily necessities' (Crawley *et al.*, 2011, p. 42).

In addition to concerns around the sexual abuse of refugee women, scholars, activists and healthcare practitioners have raised particular concerns in recent years regarding the healthcare needs of women who are pregnant and seeking asylum. Migrant women in general appear to have poorer birth outcomes than the host population, but the research does not disaggregate refugees and people seeking asylum from other migrant women (Bollini *et al.*, 2009). A systematic review of perinatal health of migrant women found that sub-Saharan African and Asian migrant women were at a greater risk of feto-infant mortality and pre-term birth than women in the host country. However, the authors note that most of the studies did not differentiate between different categories of migrants or socioeconomic status and so an accurate comparison of the studies is very difficult (Gagnon *et al.*, 2009). Perinatal mortality is a cause of concern for migrant women, particularly refugees and asylum seekers, across a range of different receiving countries (Råssjö *et al.*, 2013; Phillimore, 2015) including Sweden (Small *et al.*, 2009) and the UK (Lewis, 2007). Hannah Lewis (2007), in her report on destitution in Leeds for the Joseph Rowntree Charitable Foundation, records a particularly distressing case of a young African woman who had miscarried while destitute and had been unable to access a GP.

CASE STUDY: PREGNANT AND DESTITUTE

'I used to eat twice a day when pregnant – tea, rice, sweet potatoes. No fish or meat … I noticed a change in my body. Anyone can know … I was working two jobs, more than 50 hours. I have to lift many things. If I was living a normal life I wouldn't be working when I was pregnant … I used to get pains for two weeks. I couldn't sleep. All my body was aching … One afternoon I felt some water coming out. The person I was with said, 'you've miscarried'. That night I started bleeding. I spent the whole night on the toilet. That's when everything came out.'

When she first noticed the pains, she had procured through a friend some herbal medicine from Africa to give her strength. She rang her GP, but was told that they could not see her as she was not in staying in their area. Without ID she thought she could not register locally. She also believed she could not go to hospital, as they ask for the name of your doctor and she did not have one. Before the miscarriage she saw a friend of a friend from Africa who said he was a doctor but was not practising in the UK. Following the miscarriage she bought some Chinese medicine – herbal tea and pills – and sat at home for one month.

'I feel like I am still living in [African country] – when people have money they can go to hospitals. If I'm poorly I have to find my own way to get well.'

Even at a time of great need this woman was reluctant to access NHS healthcare. She had been told by her friend about a woman and her children going to hospital for treatment and getting deported. Before her miscarriage, she was preparing for the prospect of having her baby at home (Lewis, 2007, p. 32).

Access to healthcare is neither consistent across European countries nor groups of migrants. The legal framework that grants rights of access to healthcare varies (Bradby *et al.*, 2015). In the UK, entitlement to free healthcare was linked to immigration status in 2004. Although the NHS is free at the point of delivery for UK citizens, hospital trusts were given the statutory duty to determine the eligibility to healthcare of an 'overseas visitor' (Department of Health, 2014; 2015; 2016). Under this legislation, refused asylum seekers were no longer entitled to free secondary healthcare. Despite concerns during public and expert consultation that this was negatively impacting on health and other inequalities (Department of Health, 2013a; 2013b), the UK government extended this legislation (Department of Health, 2014). In 2015, a system for charging for NHS secondary care was introduced. Asylum seekers, people with limited leave to remain and refugees all have access to free healthcare while they remain in the asylum system, but undocumented and irregular migrants, refused asylum seekers and short-term visitors are liable to be charged healthcare costs.

In the UK, the campaigning charity Maternity Action wrote a letter in July 2018 to the Secretary of State for Health expressing concern that vulnerable migrant women were being charged between £4,000 and £10,000 for hospital maternity services. The charity claims that many of these women have lived in the UK for several years and include women who are destitute following the asylum process and/or have been brought by abusive partners (Maternity Action, 2018). Stress has been demonstrated to have long-term effects on the emotional and neurological development of children (Glover and Barlow, 2014; Kinsella and Monk, 2009), and many undocumented women are living with high levels of stress and anxiety as the result of charges for maternity services that they are never able to meet as well as from domestic violence and uncertain immigration status (Women's Health and Equity Consortium, 2017).

A recent European systematic review that looked at the impact of access and delivery of healthcare to asylum seekers and refugees found that access to healthcare is also impacted by several other factors: communication difficulties and a lack of interpreters; cultural issues such as gender preferences for a doctor; structural issues such as transport; bureaucratic systems; and insurance policies (Bradby *et al.*, 2015). The use of detention and dispersal policies was also recognised as impacting on healthcare outcomes.

The asylum system in the UK: Becoming homeless

Lived experience: Aziz's story

Aziz's story is not unusual. I met him in May 2016 at a 'food bank' I was volunteering at in England. I got to know him over a number of weeks and he told me his migration story. Well educated, and qualified as an engineer in Eritrea, Aziz wanted to work in his home country but was required to do military conscription. Falling between the strict criteria of a refugee as described under the UNHCR mandate, Aziz was not exactly an economic migrant either. He found it not too difficult to get from Eritrea to Libya as he had money and could pay for transport overland. When in Libya, he told me that it was easy to find – or be found – by people traffickers and he paid the €4,000 for the trip across the Mediterranean. He described in graphic terms the terrifying boat trip in the dark across the sea, fearing for his life on many occasions. He made it eventually, and safely, to Italian shores and then proceeded to head up to northern Europe. He still had money, so it wasn't too hard to get a ride in a truck going north through Italy, and several truck rides later he made it to Calais. I asked him on several occasions why he particularly wanted to get to the UK and he said: 'I speak English, not German' and 'I have friends in London'. Aziz described the atrocious living conditions in the Calais 'jungle' camp over the winter of 2015 and said that he'd tried on many occasions to get through at Calais to Dover. He eventually made it to the UK, although he refused to tell me exactly how he'd managed this – no matter how many times I asked!

Aziz's life since arriving in the UK and claiming asylum has been one of stress and disappointment. He ran out of money before making it to Calais and so was penniless when he arrived in the UK. Claiming asylum, he was taken under the administrative control of the NASS and allocated a room in the north-east of England. He was given £35 per week and registered with a general practitioner, but otherwise left to find his own way through the asylum system. Aziz was subsequently refused asylum by the Home Office in May 2016 and, following an appeal, was refused again and found himself evicted from his NASS house, 'sofa surfing' with friends and facing a very uncertain future in the UK.

In July 2017, Aziz found that local refugee charities were opening up opportunities for destitute guys like himself to be housed with sympathetic local families. He was introduced to an older English couple who had two spare bedrooms as their family had grown up and moved out. He lived with them for over a year. Life was again tolerable but his long-term future remains very uncertain.

As the world media carries pictures of people crossing the Mediter-ranean sea in flimsy boats, local communities receive refugees and people seeking asylum through a complex and inconsistent bureaucratic process. The UK is currently still a signatory to the 1951 Convention on Refugees and therefore is legally obliged to admit any persons seeking asylum; as such, these people are permitted to remain in the UK until their claim for asylum has been decided. In addition, the UK has also committed in 2017 to receiving a further 20,000 Syrian refugees via the UNHCR resettlement scheme. While the tabloid media use emotive language to describe the influx of refugees to the UK as a 'flood' (Gabrielatos and Baker, 2008), the reality of the numbers is somewhat different: reaching a peak of 84,592 in 2002, official government statistics indicate that 26,350 people claimed asylum in the UK in 2017 (Refugee Council, 2018).

Once admitted to the UK, people seeking asylum – from Greek ásȳlon, meaning sanctuary – are 'processed' by the Asylum Support (for-merly the NASS), which is the parallel system of welfare and support set up by the Home Office. In 2000, the Labour government responded to public and political pressure to move people who are seeking asylum away from the congested ports of entry to the UK, by instituting a system of 'dispersal'. Murphy (2009), in an exploration of homelessness in San Francisco, identified dispersal as a form of regulation that served to hide homelessness from the general public. Walby and Lippert (2011) identify dispersal in citizen homeless populations in Ottawa, Canada, as a way of policing parks and public spaces to ensure that city spaces are purified from the sight of poverty (DeVerteuil, 2006). As a consequence, people seeking asylum do not drift into UK cities, but are placed by the Home Office on a 'no choice' basis depending on housing availability and existing contracts with the Home Office. In these cities, a large network of voluntary and community sector organisations have developed to meet the needs of people seeking asylum and to plug the 'gaps' in the statutory system.

While the political rhetoric asserts that 'the UK has a proud history of providing protection to those who need it', citing the Jewish child migrants following the Second World War as a case and example, this is vociferously challenged by scholars and lobby groups alike. Kirkwood *et al.* (2016) use discourse analysis to explore narratives of asylum, and they conclude that the rhetoric of 'welcoming refugees' does not match the reality of restrictive practices in the UK. Lobby groups also challenge the 'sanctuary' thesis: Britain is one of only a few countries in Europe that uses indefinite detention for people seeking asylum and continues to detain children as part of the asylum process. The UNHCR are so concerned about detention for administrative purposes that they launched two reports as part of its 'Global strategy beyond detention 2014–2019', which aims to support governments to end the detention of asylum seekers and refugees (UNHCR, 2016b). The initial report states:

> The United Kingdom (UK) relies on and utilises detention in asylum procedures more frequently than most other countries in the EU. In 2015, of the 33,000 individuals who were detained in immigration detention, almost 15,000 were asylum-seekers. UNHCR has observed an increased reliance on the Detained Fast Track procedure (DFT) for asylum processing with approximately 15% (4,000) of the UK asylum caseload going through the procedure in 2014 and early 2015, before it was suspended by the Government in July 2015. The UK is also one of a handful of countries without a maximum time limit on immigration

detention and 2015 saw an increase in long-term detention with over 100 detainees detained for over a year (UNHCR, 2016a, p. 75).

Cleveland *et al.* (2018) describe detention as a form of structural violence. In investigating homelessness in Canada, Ali defines structural violence as:

> the social structure of society, informed largely by economic criteria related to the unequal distribution of resources and power, resulting in the constraining of individual agency of subaltern people, placing them in harm's way (Ali, 2010, p. 85).

Normally, citizens can be incarcerated only if they have committed a criminal offence, but increasingly national governments incarcerate non-criminal, non-citizens for migratory purposes and take away their rights of liberty (Edwards, 2011). The UK is one of only a few countries in the EU that does not have a time limit on detention. The campaigning group Detention Action has repeatedly challenged the UK government over the last decade on the issue, arguing strongly – with the support of some moving personal testimonies from across Europe – that detention is inhumane, futile and unjust (Vanderbruggen *et al.*, 2014). Nonetheless, the UK government acknowledges the criticisms but continues to defend the use of detention (McGuinness and Gower, 2017).

Health scholars across a range of countries have documented high levels of mental ill health, trauma, depression and self-harm caused by periods of detention (Robjant *et al.*, 2009a; Bull *et al.*, 2012; Filges *et al.*, 2016; Bosworth, 2016), and Canadian researchers found that even short periods of detention can be detrimental to mental health, eroding a sense of self (Cleveland *et al.*, 2018). A study in the UK found that 76% of detained asylum seekers were clinically depressed, compared to 26% of non-detained asylum seekers (median detention of thirty days) (Robjant *et al.*, 2009b), and even higher levels of clinical depression, anxiety and PTSD have been found in similar studies in the USA (Keller *et al.*, 2003). Cleveland *et al.* (2018) found that detained asylum seekers felt a strong sense of humiliation and disempowerment at being 'treated like criminals', while waiting for the outcomes of their legal case that they perceived as an arbitrary decision and one that they had no control over. For many people who have experienced torture and imprisonment in their own country, detention can trigger re-traumatisation (Filges *et al.*, 2016; Bosworth, 2016; Cleveland *et al.*, 2018). As time progresses in detention, mental health deteriorates (Popescu, 2016).

Many scholars and politicians in the UK argue that the asylum system is adversarial (McDonald and Billings, 2007), deeply flawed and contributes to increasing numbers of destitute people in our cities. While people are waiting for their claim for asylum to be processed, they are allocated accommodation and financial support as a weekly allowance, which is currently set at £37.75 per week for a single person over the age of eighteen years. Children are allowed to go to school and people seeking asylum have access to NHS. Nonetheless, they are prohibited from any form of employment and are not given a National Insurance number. Boredom and mental ill health are widely documented consequences of this system (Crawley *et al.*, 2011; H. Lewis, 2007). Once in the asylum system, applicants have the responsibility of 'proving' to the Home Office that they have a just and valid claim for asylum and are seeking safety from persecution. Increasingly, scholarly literature highlights the complexity of poverty, conflict, displacement and prejudice in many countries, and yet the asylum system struggles to cope with the complexity of lived experience.

The fast-track system in the UK has been particularly controversial, where decisions are made on asylum claims from certain countries within a matter of weeks. In January 2017, the UK High Court ruled that more than 10,000 asylum seekers had been treated unfairly from 2005 to 2014 and that 'detained fast track' was unlawful and beyond the power of the Home Office (Taylor, 2017). While there is scant evidence of destitution following detention, my own research exploring the experiences of destitution following the asylum system in the UK (Cuthill *et al.*, 2013) uncovered several stories of destitution following detention.

The most recent government data indicates that 28% of people seeking asylum in 2017 were granted asylum or a form of temporary protection (Refugee Council, 2018). The options for those who are refused become very limited. While families are generally allowed to remain in their accommodation until they are deported, there are many documented cases where families have been evicted from their Home Office accommodation following refusal of their asylum case and have become destitute. For some, emergency accommodation is provided under Section 4 of the Immigration and Asylum Act 1999, but this is awarded only under strict conditions, takes a long time to process and often includes voluntary return to the country of origin. Prior (2006) found that many people refuse Section 4 support, believing it to be a 'back door' to deportation to the country they fled from in the first place. For most single people and childless couples, final refusal of their asylum case results in eviction from their Home Office accommodation within twenty-one days and a request to seek voluntary return to their county of origin. While the charity Asylum Aid currently assists with voluntary return, many people do not take up this 'option', fearing that it will result in imprisonment, torture and danger on return to their country of origin.

Lived Experience: Hassan

Hassan, an Iranian national, told us how the Home Office released him from Dunvegan Detention Centre, in Scotland by taking him in a van and dropping him off in a back alley in Middlesbrough because the only address he had was of a friend in Middlesbrough, who had since been moved on.

> **'I asked where I was going and they asked where I came from. I said Middlesbrough, but I said that I didn't have a house, so they just took me in a van and opened the van door and put me out on a back street. I asked where do I sleep tonight? But they just shook their heads and left me. I have been sleeping on the streets or with my friends, when they let me, ever since.'**

Increasingly, the UK press are covering stories of EU nationals who are being detained by the police and face removal to their own country or are threatened with destitution and homelessness. The Home Office stated in its enforcement strategy that 'those not prioritised for removal [...] should be denied the benefits and privileges of life in the UK and experience an increasingly uncomfortable environment so that they elect to leave' (Home Office, 2007, p. 17). Many scholars and campaigning groups are raising concern about the increasingly 'hostile environment' deliberately created by the Home Office to remove illegal migrants from the streets of the UK. There has been a wave of media stories where EU nationals are threatened with destitution if they do not agree to return to their country of origin (Townsend, 2017a) and of the removal of 'rough sleepers' from the streets of UK cities, with the explicit intention of deportation. Fear is a constant theme running through the accounts of undocumented homeless migrants (Bloch, 2013).

In recent research I carried out in Edinburgh to explore the healthcare experiences of people who sleep rough in a Scottish city, five of the participants I interviewed (out of ten) – all foreign nationals – told me stories of their friends and acquaintances who were hiding in undisclosed secret locations around the city as they were afraid of 'being picked up by the police and deported' back to their country of origin. Of particular concern for charities working with rough sleepers, *The Guardian* newspaper claimed on 19 August 2017, was that the Home Office had been given access to a map created by the Greater London Authority (GLA) that identified and categorised rough sleepers by nationality (Townsend, 2017b). It was then able to use this map to direct officers to detain and deport rough sleepers. This follows on from the introduction of guidance by the Home Office in May 2016, enabling immigration enforcement teams to deport EU nationals, purely on the grounds that they were sleeping rough. As the numbers of visible homeless – rough sleepers – are seen on the UK streets, so the voices of those who want to remove them from the streets continue to grow.

'Invisible' and homelesss: Undocumented migrants and health

While the UK government has refused to acknowledge destitution following the asylum system, a plethora of research suggests otherwise: the experience of destitution has been extensively documented over the last fifteen years in Swansea (Crawley *et al.*, 2011); Leeds (H. Lewis, 2007); Manchester (British Red Cross and Boaz Trust, 2013); Glasgow (Hamilton and Harris, 2009; Gillespie, 2012); and Teesside (Cuthill *et al.*, 2013). The Joint Committee for Human Rights (JCHR, 2007) revealed a 'deliberate policy of refusing benefits to some asylum seekers combined with a ban on legal working left many would-be refugees in appalling circumstances'; there is little evidence to suggest this has changed in the intervening years.

The health needs of people who become homeless following the asylum process in the UK converge with the local homeless population, while also presenting particular health needs. The time between receiving the letter from the Home Office to eviction from the asylum system, and accommodation is only fifteen days, which creates intense stress and anxiety.

Each day then becomes a quest for a bed for the night and food for the day (Taylor, 2009). Soup runs are well-established transitory spaces for homeless people to find support and food (Johnsen *et al.*, 2005) and migrants make use of these, too. Many people go around third-sector organisations to get bags of food, a hot meal and/or somewhere warm to spend the night (ASAP, 2008). Libraries are frequently used as places of refuge from the cold and somewhere to access the internet for free. At this stage in the asylum process, people have no rights and NRPF. The only 'offer' by the Home Office is voluntary return to their country of origin. Nonetheless, many argue that this is not possible, as they claim they will face certain detention, imprisonment and torture on return. Others have lost contact with family members because of war and conflict and have nothing, or no one, to return to in their country of origin. Others have no official documentation and are refused entry by the country they claim to be from. The issue of 'burning passports' as a means of no-return has been widely reported in the press as a means to stay in a safe country.

For people who have NRPF, they are unable to access the usual homeless hostels, B&B accommodation or homeless shelters, as these are available only to people who are eligible for welfare support. Day centres rarely differentiate between the local homeless population and people with NRPF, so many people use these to wash clothes, access the internet and get a warm cup of tea. Nonetheless, the problem of where to stay each night becomes acute. People frequently 'sofa-surf' with people they know from their country, but that can put the accommodation provision of friends in jeopardy if the Home Office discovers someone not authorised in the accommodation.

In my many years of working with people who are destitute following the asylum process, I have heard stories of people sleeping on the floors of pizza shops in return for unpaid labour; sleeping in bus shelters and alleyways; of walking around the city all night and sleeping in a friend's bed during the day; and of a myriad other ways to keep safe and warm.

The health needs of people who find themselves destitute following the asylum system have been well documented by scholars (H. Lewis, 2007; Crawley et al., 2011; Cuthill et al., 2013) but are largely ignored by government bodies. Mental health needs are related to the crisis of people finding themselves refused asylum and a strong sense of injustice that their 'case' has not been successful. The asylum system itself is recognised as a source of stress and anxiety. After escaping poverty, war, violence and danger, many people enter high-income countries expecting sanctuary, and find themselves homeless and living on the streets, barred from working and without any recourse to public funds. In addition, anxiety about the future and the boredom of filling each day with no future map takes its toll on mental health. Underlying PTSD and anxiety disorders are intensified by the lack of safety and security, coupled with the stress of an uncertain future. Social isolation, a lack of hope for the future and poverty have a compounding impact on mental health. For many people, anxiety over the fate of family members back in their country of origin and concern over the future intensifies feelings of loneliness and isolation. Sleep disturbances and memory loss are common experiences (Burnett and Peel, 2001).

Physically, people are often hungry and lack appropriate nutritional intakes. Often missing meals and experiencing inadequate nutrition, people become susceptible to infection. This is exacerbated by people living together in overcrowded accommodation to avoid a life on the streets. As a consequence, people are at risk of transmission of infectious diseases such as TB, respiratory infections, gastroenteritis and skin conditions (lice and scabies) (Semenza *et al.*, 2016). People walk long distances to access food banks and third-sector organisations for meals. While many people seeking asylum and refugees do not drink alcohol for religious reasons, scholars have documented how people can turn to alcohol and drug use as a coping strategy (Dupont *et al.*, 2005). Many people report musculoskeletal problems, which manifest as sore backs, limbs and headaches, and are associated with emotional distress, trauma and tension (Burnett and Peel, 2001).

Health and welfare needs of people who are homeless following the asylum process are met in a haphazard and opportunistic way. Much has been debated about access to primary healthcare services and, while many specialist services do not ask about legal 'status' in the country and treat people at the point of need, there have been many cases where people have been turned away from GP services once they are beyond the asylum system. This lack of access to healthcare services exacerbates healthcare needs. In addition, many people have experiences in their home country of healthcare services colluding with government agencies, and so are very suspicious of primary healthcare services and will not access them for fear of detention and deportation.

While working as a community nurse for people seeking asylum and refugees, I have known so many people who managed their mental and physical health needs prior to being evicted from their property, and then following a path where their health and well-being plummeted downwards into physical ill health, harmful substance use and 'rough sleeping'. For the most vulnerable, eviction from the home can lead to a very precarious life on the streets that is compounded by difficulties with language, culture and access to services. In many ways, the most vulnerable people exist in a shadow world, ignored by state agencies as non-citizens and yet must exist in our cities as 'living ghosts'. Exploitation and forced labour are common experiences as people try to survive (Lewis and Waite, 2015).

While scholars initially focused research on men who were made homeless following the asylum process, the scholarly lens has turned in recent years to explore the experiences of groups who are more hidden – women and child migrants. Women have their own vulnerabilities when they are made homeless following the asylum system. Being at high risk of sexual abuse and exploitation, many are known to survive through intimate relationships and sex work. This leads to a high risk of gender-based violence and abuse.

Lived experience: Safia's story

I remember clearly the Christmas Eve, 24 December 2010, when I met a woman who was seven months pregnant and had been evicted from her property two days previously by the Home Office following the determination of her asylum case and refusal. A Sudanese national, she had left Sudan with her husband but they had become separated during transit and she was now alone in a foreign country and homeless. She had two other children who had been left with her mother and wider family in Sudan, and she was traumatised by the separation. When I met Safia, she was distraught as she had nowhere to go, services and charities were about to close for Christmas and she spoke very limited English. The day was very cold and we were very concerned about her mental health, emotional distress and her unborn baby.

Conclusion

In this chapter, homelessness is framed as the consequence of global conflict, forced migration, political pressure and government policy, where the displaced migrant finds that they are experiencing homelessness and living without recourse to public funds at the end of a long and unending road to find safety, security and a home in a new land. The physical, mental and emotional needs of people seeking asylum and refugees are different at each stage of the refugee 'journey' and can be specific, depending on gender and age. Health needs intensify considerably following a refusal of their asylum case, and people are forced into homelessness as they become undocumented migrants and are charged for healthcare that they will never be able to pay. Nonetheless, despite the trauma and undeniable hardship experienced by many forced migrants, the story is not all negative and one of brokenness and vulnerability. There is also incredible strength and resilience in the face of adversity. While some people do move into harmful substance use and a life on the streets, many do not and find ingenious and inventive ways to survive, if not quite thrive. Chapter 4 focuses on resilience and resistance in the harshest of circumstances, arguing that refugee lives are not only a story of vulnerability and brokenness, but also one of triumph and strength through adversity.

CHAPTER 4

Keeping Strong: Resilience and resistance as health assets

In recent years, an asset-based approach to public health has gained traction, focusing on resilience for health rather than on health deficits. While this is now evidenced in UK government policy, it has been slower to be explored in research around homelessness and health. Nonetheless, several studies in recent years have uncovered resilience and resistance by those who are homeless, and research has uncovered the ways that identity, stigma and societal discourses support resilience in destitution. This chapter will draw on theory and research from a range of fields including urban studies, geography and sociology to explore the contours of resilience and resistance in homelessness. This critical approach invites practitioners and policymakers to uncover new ways of conceptualising homelessness and health to become better informed about the role of identity in care practice.

Counter-narratives of vulnerability

As highlighted already, there is a significant amount of research into the health needs of people who experience homelessness that focuses on vulnerability, death and disease. This sits well with campaigning attempts to highlight the high mortality and morbidity rates of homeless people to secure funding and resources. Indeed, the adverse impact of homelessness on health is wide and deep, and the details will be explored further in Chapter 5. Nonetheless, people who experience homelessness are presented overwhelmingly in the healthcare literature as broken, vulnerable, fragile and living precarious lives. Devereux (2015) highlights the Christmas appeals of many homelessness charities and the ways that making homelessness visible as a 'human interest' story can obscure the complex interplay of individual agency and structural inequalities and 'in fact serve to further circulate hackneyed well-worn understandings of homelessness which do little to challenge existing assumptions or purpose long term solutions' (Devereux, 2015, p. 262). These discourses of vulnerability are shaped by society in several interconnecting ways: by the media, where homelessness is represented by the middle-aged alcoholic man sleeping in shop doorways or the illegal immigrant; by public health discourses, where homelessness is treated as a risk factor to be managed and eradicated; by NGOs, charities and community organisations, which are required to present a narrative of vulnerability in order to secure funding or public sympathy (see Devereux, 2015 for further discussion); and by people who experience homelessness themselves, as they learn to 'fit their individual narrative into an extended political discourse' (Pineteh, 2005, p. 383).

Drawing on the seminal work of Goffman (1967, rev. edn 2009), I found this in my own research where both refugees and refugee organisations played scripted roles, accentuating vulnerability and silencing narratives of resilience, in order to gain citizenship (Cuthill, 2017). They were keen to represent themselves politically and yet had very limited levers available to get their voices heard (Cuthill, 2016). This concurs with Rosello's (2012) analysis of modern literature that represents refugee lives, where the 'the asylum seeker's narrative performance opens or shuts the border by establishing the refugee's identity' (Rosello, 2012, p. 5). In such a harsh and increasingly 'hostile' political landscape, people experiencing homelessness are required to present themselves as vulnerable in order to secure the help of services, organisations and individuals. Despite multiple attempts by frontline workers, researchers, activists and people with lived experience to present a different narrative and to frame homelessness in different ways (Frameworks Institute, 2017; O'Neill *et al.*, 2016), these visual and oral stories of vulnerability, death and disease remain persistent and narratives of strength in adversity are rare in healthcare discourse.

Nonetheless, while discourses of vulnerability have many threads of reality, they are not the whole picture. 'Everyday resistance' is found in the ways that people who live with the consequences of inequality shape their lives to resist oppression (De Certeau, 1984). In a study of TB and homelessness in Toronto, Canada, Ali (2010) found that individual agency was mediated through 'structural violence' on the streets. Research originating in the field of urban studies and the built environment has focused on ways in which the uneven distribution of power evident in the neoliberal project is replicated in the streets of individual cities. Davis (1990) describes vividly the polarisation of urban spaces into areas where the homeless are increasingly contained and herded into ever decreasing corrals in LA. This was refined by Smith (2001) who conceptualised the city in terms of urban revanchism (vengeance). Smith (2001) goes on to argue that zero tolerance policies by the police were designed to clear rough sleepers from prime city spaces to the periphery. Both of these accounts by Davis (1990) and Smith (2001) have become powerful narratives of urban homelessness. Nonetheless, Cloke *et al.* (2010) present a much more nuanced vision of homelessness within both urban and rural spaces. While recognising that homelessness can be seen as the result of powerful structural forces in society, these discourses deny the agency of the individual: to resist, to be resilient and to express alternative social and political ideologies in the city. Furthermore, the role of charity workers, healthcare professionals and volunteers around the city are re-envisioned as not merely agents of a repressive state, but also as a complex mixture of human motivation (Cloke *et al.*, 2010). Contesting the revanchist orthodoxy, these workers are seen as resisting the pressure from state organisations.

Representing citizen and non-citizen homelessness in the media

When studying the field of homelessness and health, several different lenses can be used to frame the issues, but most commonly the biomedical and public health approaches are used. While these serve to illuminate certain important aspects of the debate, they can leave unexamined the ways that society, the media, politics and organisations structure, and are structured by, societal discourses. Poverty, destitution and homelessness are nothing new and can be traced from medieval times to the current day (Crisis, 2017), but the subject of homelessness has gained political and policy traction in recent years in the UK and USA. Upton (2016) and Wacquant (2009) take a political economy approach to foreground the ways that 'homelessness' is being reframed as a political and historical subject in the USA. Certainly, many scholars see a renewed interest in the ways that social problems have become politicised in recent years (Beck, 2015), especially issues surrounding public space (Fainstein, 2010).

It is helpful to look at the sociological literature as a way to 'reveal what is hidden' (Bourdieu, 2011, p. 17). Sociological scholars have led the way in interrogating the emergence of such labels as 'homelessness' and the ways that homelessness is socially constructed (Cronley, 2010), which includes an interrogation of the ways that narratives of homelessness are mediated through the media and policy discourses. Several scholars have since sought to interrogate historically how such labels as 'homelessness' have emerged. DeVerteuil *et al.* (2009) assert that the 'homeless city' is an urban space where poverty management is operationalised from such wide-ranging actors as third-sector support to punitive management and, in this context, 'homelessness' has re-emerged as a policy focus when issues of poverty and deprivation are less in the headlines.

Certainly, many scholars see homelessness as a shorthand for poverty, and indeed, as Upton (2016) argues, current discourse focuses on 'homelessness' rather than 'poverty' because it can be framed as a social problem that is easier to solve than the broader, more diffuse social issue of poverty. The study of homelessness can have a number of entry points, the majority being the person experiencing homelessness themselves, but several authors start with 'us' rather than 'them'. Likewise, Kendall (2005) has explored framing in relation to social class in North America and has highlighted that homelessness was much more widely reported than health inequalities and poverty in general. She asserts that this is because the experience of homelessness garners more sympathy or is perceived as easier to solve. In 1966, Becker suggested that 'the definition of a problem usually contains, implicitly or explicitly, suggestions of how it may be solved' (Becker, 1966, p. 10). In continuing this line of argument, Cronley (2010) highlights how much research is focused on explaining the causes of homelessness, and the hope is that this will then lead to prevention and intervention strategies. While the motives of individual researchers or teams of researchers are admirable to identify pathways into homelessness in order to solve this as a social problem, critical scholars have pointed out the ways that this can also serve to construct 'the homeless' as a problematic category of people to control (Gerrard and Farrugia, 2015).

The core tension at the heart of the debate around homelessness is that it is described simultaneously as a 'wicked problem', complex and multifaceted, and as a problem that can be solved by identifying the entry and exit points and is straightforward if enough homes are provided. The charity Crisis have been driving the agenda forward in the UK (Crisis, 2018), and in Scotland in particular, where homelessness is framed as unfair, unjust and a problem to be solved (Scottish Government, 2018a). While this approach is welcomed by charities, healthcare practitioners in the sector and people who are sleeping outdoors in the winter months, it can obscure the ways that the welfare state gives with one hand and takes away with the other (Wacquant, 2009). As the Scottish media reported cuts to drug and alcohol services by the Scottish government in 2016/17 and funding transferred to the NHS (Naysmith, 2016), the Scottish government announced £50 million to end rough sleeping in the winter of 2017/18. Again, narratives of rough sleeping and homelessness are conflated, and increasing visibility of people sleeping on the streets of Edinburgh, Glasgow and Aberdeen has triggered a strong policy response. Figures for statutory homelessness in Scotland have reduced year on year since 2010 (National Statistics for Scotland, 2018), and yet the increased visibility of people sleeping rough in recent years has triggered government action. Noting a similar phenomenon in the USA, Upton (2016, p.3) cites several examples where 'cities respond to visible indicators of homelessness, such as encampments and tent cities as indicative of rising homelessness, even if statistical data does not indicate this'. She points out that homelessness has recently been reframed as a State of Emergency (SoE) in several areas: Los Angeles, Oakland, Eugene, Hawaii and Seattle. This was triggered by figures demonstrating increased homelessness in the USA – in New York and California in particular – and the framing of a 'catastrophe of homelessness' by the NGO, the Coalition of Homelessness (2016). Upton (2016) presents a convincing argument of the ways that this then triggers economic support and financial priority to these states. Whether homelessness is hidden or is even made visible as a social problem can influence policymakers (Best, 2010).

Policymakers and researchers are keen to develop a robust evidence base to find out 'what works' to end homelessness (Centre for Homelessness Impact, 2018) and:

> multiple coalitions, organizations, and alliances centred on ending homelessness fall in line with the argument that the role of the expert has been created that furthers state power and extends control (Upton, 2016, p. 6).

Upton (2016, p. 6) argues that a 'new logic of social control' has emerged that 'conflates moral and political urgency to legitimatize state intervention'.

This has been seen in Scotland in recent years, where many different coalitions have been formed around homelessness and harmful substance use, and a variety of research-based centres around homeless and inclusion health have been set up. I acknowledge that my own work is part of this clamour towards ending homelessness and improving the health and well-being of people who experience homelessness.

The way that homelessness is socially constructed and politically influenced tells us much about our world. 'Media content provides us with the many "scripts" necessary for us to negotiate and make sense of the everyday social contexts in which we find ourselves' (Devereux, 2015, p. 266). Wacquant (2009) has developed a strong analysis of the welfare state in a global context, arguing that welfare retrenchment and penal expansion serve the rise of the neoliberal state. Using the dismantling of the welfare state in the USA in the 1970s onwards as an example, Wacquant (2009) argues that there has been a shift towards 'neoliberal governance' and a punitive management of the poor. Building on Wacquant's (2009) concept of state control of the poor, research by Crossley (2016) in the UK on 'troubled families' uncovered the ways that increased politicisation of the poor and vulnerably housed results in further social control. Wacquant (2009) asserts that the rise in incarceration rates in the USA are a manifestation of the move by the neoliberal state to manage society's homeless, urban, poor black men.

As O'Neill (2010) and others have pointed out, the public learn to understand the lives of people who are pushed to the margins of society through the media, rather than through personal experience or through advocacy groups. Increasingly in a global neoliberal age, the media has become commodified and held in the hands of a decreasing number of media outlets, concentrating power and political influence in the hands of the few. The media is therefore 'crucially implicated in the politics of representation' (O'Neill, 2010, p. 125). This is particularly accentuated with people who live on the margins of society: gypsies and travellers; people seeking asylum and refugees; people experiencing homelessness; and people discharged from prison. The media using discursive strategies to locate the 'deserving' and the 'underserving' poor as oppositional can be traced back to the 1970s, where North American news agencies turned their lens on people experiencing homelessness (Buck *et al.*, 2004). Ravenhill (2014) asserts that the way homelessness is framed as a social problem, either as 'deserving' or the 'underserving', is reflected in the ways that homelessness is normalised, managed or corrected. Interventions are created depending on the categories that people fit.

The media is important in debates around homelessness as it not only shapes public opinion, but also the responses of policymakers (Devereux, 2015). Nonetheless, the media is never neutral – despite claims by journalists to such impartiality – and has the power to shape public discourses around homelessness, destitution and citizenship. Fenton (2011) highlights how the introduction of new media technologies in recent years had brought the hope of increasing democracy but argues that it has resulted in the rationalisation of journalism and fewer resources for critical journalism. The result, he asserts, has had a negative impact on the mainstream media and much more on desk-based journalism. In an analysis for the network news in North America from 1980 to 1993, Shields (2001, p. 194) found that 'the standard news frames construct the homeless as deviant, fortifying the boundaries between "us" and "them"'. In addition, populist politicians express concern for 'our own' homeless, in contrast to the non-citizen homeless.

The majority of research exploring the media portrayal of citizens experiencing homelessness is undertaken in North America, while non-citizen homelessness, specifically destitution following the asylum process, is more common in the UK, Europe and Australia. In Canada, Calder *et al.* (2011) carried out an analysis of thirty-eight newspaper articles between 2000 and 2010 and found that people experiencing homelessness were framed in six different ways: sympathetic; deviance; conflict; dependence; attributions; and seasonal. Frames are 'a specific set of expectations used to make sense of some aspect of the social world in a specific situation and time' (Baran and Davis, 2008, p. 282). A story might have several frames, but one frame in particular may dominate. The important aspect of frames is that there are things that are made visible and aspects that remain hidden. Calder *et al.* (2011) identify several reasons why journalists might ignore certain aspects of homelessness from the frame: for example, that the power of the press is held increasingly by fewer news agencies; that journalists do not like to go out and interview people experiencing homelessness; and that journalists increasingly come from graduates who uphold the ideology of the powerful and so the same narratives are told. McQuail (2005, p. 300) argues that this is 'because they can be trusted to see and interpret the world in much the same way as the real holders of power, holding the same basic ideology and values'.

While people seeking asylum and refugees occupy the same city spaces as the citizen experiencing homelessness, they have lost the 'right to have rights' (Arendt, 1973). In being reduced to a 'bare life' (Agamben, 1998; Darling, 2009), people seeking asylum not only occupy marginal spaces in society, but also are increasingly viewed by society as a threat to national identity (Tyler, 2006). In such a harsh political context, 'the voices of destitute asylum seekers are rarely heard' (O'Neill and Hubbard, 2012, p. 4) and, as powerfully argued by Tyler (2013), asylum seekers are presented as the 'revolting subjects' of society.

Certainly, many scholars see the media portrayal of refugees and asylum seekers as attempts by neoliberal societies to mark out lines of national and ethnic belonging (Tyler, 2006), and the sovereignty of the state. This is a key theme in the Australian literature, where the focus on the media portrayal of asylum seekers and refugees arriving by boat is framed within neoliberal discourses of economic threat and national boundaries. Discourses of the 'deserving' refugee and the 'undeserving' boat person or illegal immigrant have been identified particularly in the Australian media (O'Docherty and Lecouteur, 2007). Parker (2015), in an analysis of forty articles in the UK and Australian print media between 2001 and 2010, found that the Australian media particularly constructed discourses of border protection, whereas in the UK the focus was much more on the removal of undeserving asylum seekers. Lueck *et al.* (2015) go further by arguing that the representation of asylum seekers in the Australian media is negatively represented as a threat to economic stability in an attempt to maintain the (White) homogenous nation state. Devereux (2015) contends that:

> media content which is purportedly about 'them' is more often than not really more about 'us' in that it circulates discourses which are comforting to the majority and which fail to challenge unequal relationships of power or suggest alternatives that might threaten or destabilise the *status quo* (Devereux, 2015, p. 267; italics in original).

What is very clear in any examination of the literature exploring the representation of asylum seekers and refugees in the media, in the context of the UK and Australia particularly, is that there has been a common use of metaphors of 'tides', 'swamp' and 'flood' since asylum seekers were perceived as a problem in the late 1990s (Pickering, 2001; Khosravinik, 2009). This trend is also seen in analysis of speeches by right-wing politicians in the UK (Charteris-Black, 2006).

A significant amount of research over the last decade in the UK shows that there has been increasing competition between right-wing tabloid newspapers to publish the most hostile stories about refugees and asylum seekers in order to sell newspapers (Greenslade, 2005). Greenslade, in a historical analysis of the coverage of asylum issues in the UK press, found that the:

> drip-drip-drip of negative stories and alarmist headlines in papers
> that command the attention of a huge swathe of the adult British
> population cannot but have a negative impact on public opinion
> (Greenslade, 2005, p. 29).

This intensified during the UK general election in 2015, where the focus shifted to the 'luxurious life' that many people seeking asylum were apparently living, with the *Daily Express* splashing headlines such as 'It's good but I don't like the food says asylum seeker: 130 migrants use top hotel' (Sheldrick, 2014).

What is clear in both local citizen and migrant narratives of homelessness is that media coverage fails to interrogate the structural causes of homelessness (Hodgetts *et al.*, 2006) and focuses on the moral weakness of the individual themselves (McKendrick *et al.*, 2008). Devereux (2015) takes a political economy standpoint and argues that this focus on individual weakness, rather than structural inequality, is then used as a policy tool to reduce funding to substance use recovery programmes, to deregulate housing markets and to cut welfare benefits. Citizens who find themselves homeless are predominantly portrayed as experiencing drug or alcohol dependence, mental health issues or as criminals – a threat to the moral and social order. In the 1990s, Lind and Danowski (1999) studied portrayals of homelessness on the TV and radio in the USA and found that it was predominantly linked with mental illness, substance use and HIV/AIDS. The non-citizen homeless is represented as the illegal migrant, the criminal and the terrorist within.

The core tension at the heart of the debate is how to frame narratives of resistance and resilience as a strength of humanity, while not playing into the hands of a powerful media who conflate issues of migration, citizenship and terrorism. The construction of the homeless as the 'deviant other' is well documented, but in the area of destitution following the asylum process this is particularly politicised, and the debate seems to be intensifying. Parker's (2015) analysis presents the British and Australian media as evoking a dualism between the 'unwanted invader' and those who are 'tragic figures', with little room for the nuances, realities and complexities of lived experience.

Resilience and resistance: Asset-based approaches to health and homelessness

Despite the strong media focus on negative aspects of refugee lives, there is a strong evidence base to indicate resilience and resistance by refugees to these portrayals. In recent years, there has been a resurgence of the idea in the public health literature that resilience and assets are an important aspect of health (De Andrade, 2016). This changing of the tilt of the lens to focus on assets, rather than deficits, has opened up a space in the healthcare literature to explore the experiences of people who find themselves homeless and the strengths that they exhibit, rather than the deficits that they experience. This literature is growing in both the refugee literature and the citizen homelessness field. The focus of much of this literature is on mental health and the benefits of self-determination to mental health, including notions of identity, community and well-being. Historical accounts of homelessness demonstrate the ways that encampments, such as skid rows in the mid-twentieth century, served as centres for support and resistance (Kusmer, 2002). Smaller studies have explored the ways that people use relationships to support resilience in encampments (Langegger and Koester, 2017).

What is very clear in any examination of the global literature of both citizen and non-citizen homelessness is that there are many examples of resilience, resistance and strength waiting to be told (Hall, 2015a; 2015b; Moxley *et al.*, 2012). Resistance to the vulnerability discourse has come from several different directions: research in the field of healthcare is beginning to highlight the resilience and strength of those who are marginalised through asset-based approaches to health and well-being; homeless people are increasingly engaging in arts-based projects to assert their agency through poetry, theatre, film and dance (Streetwise Opera, 2018); residents in excluded communities are accessing media training to challenge negative stereotypes (Mutere *et al.*, 2014); and people with lived experience of homelessness are becoming integral to the health and well-being of their peers through peer-led participatory action research (Abdulkadir *et al.*, 2016). Examples of resilience are shown to operate in the lives of people marginalised across many varied and divergent landscapes: Groot and Hodgetts (2015) took a case-study approach and followed the life of Joshua, a man who used begging as a source of income generation to feed his family and to build self-worth on the street in Auckland, New Zealand; Swanson (2010) conducted an in-depth ethnographic study to reveal the subtle ways that indigenous women in Ecuador used begging to support their families; Ruddick (1996) documented how homeless young people evaded police and developed oppositional identities in the USA; and Rosa (2016) recognised the ways that the Roma in Turin, Italy used begging to recover waste and roamed the city as acts of resilience and resistance. In exploring migrant urbanisms, Hall (2015b) shows the ways that migrants and citizens in Peckham, London intersect in micro-ways to shape the city and to demonstrate 'everyday resistance' to bureaucratic intervention. Rankin *et al.* (2015) likewise document the multiple transactions that happen in a diverse shopping area in Toronto, where people trade 'under the radar'. Hall (2015b, p. 859) notes that 'this city-making emerges out of ingenuity and precarity and accommodates many sorts of newcomers'. The landscape is changing: the agency, strength and resilience of people who find themselves homeless is taking on a new shape and visibility and the role of agency and self-worth is becoming visible in healthcare literature.

Some of the overt ways that people living marginalised lives are re-framing their experiences are through the arts and sport:

- With One Voice, a collaborative of organisations connecting the arts and homelessness worldwide, is involved with some amazing initiatives around the world.
- Theatre of the Oppressed in New York City is a group that uses arts to influence policy through drama that challenges policy directives;
- Cocoroom in Osaka, Japan has developed a University of the Arts that has more than sixty workshops with everything from singing to calligraphy to develop talent and to give opportunities to flourish;

- WAYout in Freetown, Sierra Leone is a film-making group of street kids that develop media outputs, poetry and music;
- Choir of Hard Knocks in Melbourne, Australia is a group of people who live marginalised lives and have performed to sell-out audiences in the Sydney Opera House;
- With One Voice in San Paulo, Brazil demonstrates the power of coming together and cross-cultural learning through singing together.

In 2017 in London, the One Festival of Homeless Arts was held, which showcased the lives of homeless people by people who have experienced homelessness. As Matt Peacock, CEO of With One Voice, said recently at the launch of the With One Voice review of the arts and homelessness in Scotland: 'talent is everywhere but opportunity is not'. Organisations such as With One Voice give the opportunity for talent to flourish, even if it has been born in the most marginalised places, give people routes to self-expression and act as bridges for understanding into communities.

In this 2018 review of the arts and homelessness in Scotland, the peer authors conclude that Scotland has a rich and diverse arts and homelessness sector, with a breadth of innovative projects (Coyne, 2018). At the time of the report, there were understood to be twenty-three projects delivering work in Scotland.

While the arts is one way to demonstrate resilience and resistance to dominant 'vulnerability' narratives, sport is increasingly another. The Homeless World Cup has been instrumental in promoting a positive image of people experiencing homelessness and engaging in competitive sport and, in Scotland, Street Soccer Scotland has a high profile and aims to achieve positive change through football (Street Soccer Scotland, 2018). Recent research has also shown the multiple ways that football can increase self-confidence and develop capabilities in young people who are experiencing, or who are at risk of, homelessness (Ahrens, 2016).

Conclusion

In this chapter, I have argued that the media portrayal of 'the homeless' as 'vulnerable' and 'needy', or as a 'threat within' requires a reconsideration in the health literature to ensure that strengths and assets are realised, talents are harnessed, self-esteem is fostered and, in doing so, health and well-being are improved. While the mass media predominantly portrays refugee and homeless lives as broken and damaged, there is a strong body of evidence demonstrating resilience and resistance, particularly through the arts and sport, and this should be fostered and proclaimed in order to shift the frame and to support resilience and to build on existing individual and community assets to improve health and well-being.

CHAPTER 5

Prevention, Policy and Practitioners: A public health response

Neil Hamlet and Katy Hetherington

This chapter will draw on the recent public health response to homelessness in Scotland and explore the ways that policy and practice can impact on those who are 'multiply excluded' in our communities. It will interrogate the policy context, and will compare and contrast this with other similar countries in Europe. It will reflect on the successes and limitations of a range of policy approaches to public health and suggest best practice outcomes.

What is a public health approach?

Everything we see and everything we think is unconsciously channelled through a lens of our chosen profession and a filter of our upbringing and experiences. So what exactly are the lenses and filters that are applied when we adopt a 'public health approach'? In the UK public health medicine is nested within the medical establishment as the Faculty of Public Health of the Royal College of Physicians in London, which defines the specialty as: 'The science and art of promoting and protecting health and well-being, preventing ill-health and prolonging life through the organised efforts of society' (Faculty of Public Health, 2016).

So what then defines the public health mindset? Here are a few of the commonly applied lenses.

Population based

While clinical specialties operate on an individual patient-by-patient basis, the public health professional will address issues at a population or subpopulation level. The 'patient' is a community formed by gender, geography, occupation or any other shared experience. And it is society which jointly provides the solutions necessary to deliver equitable promotion, protection and extension of well-being for all.

Denominator based
Public health is all about comparisons across and between populations. How much more or less does wellness dwell or illness strike between one group of the population and another? Public health doctors are 'denominator doctors'.

Rooted in epidemiology
Epidemiology is the study of the distribution and determinants of health-related states or events in specified populations, and the application of this study to control health problems (Last et al., 2001). The point to note is that the public health mindset emphasises the interpretation, or diagnosis, demanding a response or treatment plan for the population under study. True public health requires action beyond observation and interpretation.

Underpinned by social justice and human rights
Equity of access to, delivery of and outcomes from the healthcare system is a cross-cutting theme in any public health study. Health inequality is all too common, and thus much attention is paid to reducing the burden of ill health being carried unequally across society.

Seeking the causes of the causes of the consequences
Sometimes described as 'looking upstream', effective public health digs to the root issues that lead to the behaviours that result in physical or psychological pathologies. Thus social determinants of health and risk factors – both protective and destructive – are essential aspects to consider. Our political, cultural, social and physical environments all play into the expression of our personal genetics, which together define the health experience.

Defining health and homelessness
The public health approach requires clear definitions understood by all from the outset. So what do we understand by the term 'health' and what do we mean when we talk about 'homelessness'?

Health

This is so much more that absence of illness. It is best visualised as a state within which individuals flourish and are enabled to 'be all they can be'. It is possible to have excellent physical health yet be miserable, and vice versa, to live with a long-standing condition or disability and excel in living life to the max. WHO defines 'health' as: 'A state of complete physical, mental and social well-being and not merely the absence of disease or infirmity' (WHO, 2018c).

'Health' is a word a bit like 'love' – it can carry so many meanings that it hardly has purpose anymore. I prefer the term 'wellbeing', which portrays the sense of purposeful internal peace alongside sufficiently functional physical and mental processes, resulting in an external vibrant enthusiasm for living life in the now.

Another clarification is required when using the terms 'health', as now defined above, and 'healthcare' which describes all aspects of the provision of services to assist with a perceived lack of 'health'. The NHS is actually in large measure a national sickness treatment service and possesses limited budget for upstream illness prevention and health-promoting activities. With the laudable attempts at integration of social care and healthcare, Scotland now has Health and Social Care Partnerships (HSCPs) largely covering local authority areas. It is these bodies that have most to contribute to the prevention and mitigation of both the causes of and the consequences arising from the condition we call 'homelessness'.

Homelessness

This is yet another overused term infused and confused by our preconceptions, which range from the 'vagabond' or more modern 'down and out' to the occasional sofa-surfer. Because most societies provide some form of social safety net for those without a safe place to shelter, a definition of who is homeless is essential for the state to be able to set legislation on that service provision. And as each state – even across the four devolved nations of the UK – takes a different stance on that provision, the legal definition of homelessness varies accordingly. Work is currently underway by the UK Office of National Statistics (ONS) to seek agreement on 'what is homelessness' and it is not proving an easy task. International bodies offer helpful nomenclature in the sub-classification of homelessness across the span of conditions or states which can be best grouped as forms of 'insecure housing' (see page vii for FEANTSA and *Homeless Monitor* definitions).

Finally on the use of definitions and descriptions in a human rights informed age, it is pertinent to revisit the term the 'homeless' as an appropriate societal categorisation for today. We never label the injured as the 'broken-legged' or the 'car-crashed', nor use terms such as the 'cancer-ed' or the 'pregnant' in society. Why then do we freely talk about the 'homeless'? Perhaps there should be no place to define people based on their current, passing or past physical or sociological state of being. Surely we are now sufficiently sensitive to the language of interpersonal respect and human rights to coin the phrase 'people who experience homelessness'. If we have moved from 'drug mis-users' to 'people who inject drugs' then now is the time to introduce a suitable non-stigmatising acronym for those who experience a phase of homelessness in their lives.

The roots of public health

If we look back to the origins of what have now become the very separate professions of housing studies and public health we discover their strongly linked parentage in the impact of the industrial revolution on the burgeoning towns and the associated housing squalor and rampant disease of the mid-1800s.

In 1854 a man by the name of John Snow removed the handle from the well in Broad Street in London, and the cholera outbreak subsided. And so was born the science of epidemiology upon which the science and art of public health practice depends. The dramatic impact of public health practice in its early forms was in the improvements of the physical built environment – essentially town planning – for the well-being of the burgeoning city populace. In 1865 Dr Henry Littlejohn, Scotland's first municipal officer of health, published his report on the sanitary conditions of the city of Edinburgh. The link between (poor) housing and (poor) well-being could not have been more evident.

One year earlier, in 1864, a genteel Victorian lady by the name of Octavia Hill threw herself into visiting the factory working class in their squalid London housing conditions. This social welfare approach became what is now know as housing studies. and Hill is immortalised to housing practitioners as John Snow is to public health. Truly housing and public health were born for each other.

This close link between public health and housing is also seen at early structural levels within government. In was only in 1951 that the joint portfolio of housing and health under one government ministry was separated. The 1919 Housing & Town Planning Act, to create 'homes fit for heroes', introduced the concept of social rented housing for the masses, and an ambitious programme of house building was commenced. We must never forget the elephant in the corner of the social housing sector: namely that of sufficient houses of appropriate size, location and quality available at affordable rent for those who find themselves without a home and fallen from the lowest rung of the housing ladder to which we have been taught to aspire.

Public health today

The resurgence of public health engagement with housing and homelessness in Scotland will be described later in the chapter; however two areas of work are likely to hold major implications for the next decade. These are the adoption of national priorities for public health, and the growing acknowledgement of the importance of ACEs in society.

The Scottish government, together with the Confederation of Scottish Local Authorities (COSLA) have produced a set of public health priorities for Scotland (Scottish Government, 2018c). It is recognised within these priorities that, to improve the health of the Scottish population and address health inequalities, action is required much wider than healthcare and social care. This begins with a deeper focus on the homes and communities where people live. Collaborative working, with communities, is recognised as essential if this vision is to be achieved. The first priority identified is listed as 'a Scotland where we live in vibrant, healthy and safe places and communities'. Within this is recognition of the importance of connections, and it is in homes where individuals develop their first relationships as babies, children and young people and which can set the path for future health and well-being.

The ACE study (Felitti *et al.*, 1998) found from a large population survey that as the number of adverse events occurring within a child's life increased, so did links with later health and well-being issues. The events included direct ones such as emotional, physical and sexual abuse, physical and emotional neglect, and also experiences going on in the home including substance abuse, mental illness, domestic violence, divorce or parental separation and a household member going to prison. Further ACE studies, including within the UK, have replicated findings. The stress experienced in our early years can have lifelong impacts on our health and well-being. Research into the body's stress response system is giving us a better understanding of how adversity can affect our bodies (Burke-Harris, 2018). Providing a safe, stable home environment for children within which they can grow, learn and trust those who are caring for them is a public health 'intervention'. Creating salutogenic homes is clearly about providing the bricks and mortar for a house as well as fostering the right conditions for adults and families to provide a safe and stable environment for children to thrive and reach their full potential (Burke-Harris, 2018).

NHS and homelessness in Scotland
The power of politics and politicians
At the time of devolution (1998) and the formation of the first Scottish Parliament, homelessness agencies and third-sector bodies successfully lobbied the incoming new Members of the Scottish Parliament (MSPs) to take a stand on the issue of the health of the homeless and the role of NHS Boards in tackling the issue. This led directly to the formation of a Health and Homelessness Steering Group and the first ever *Health and Homelessness Guidance* (NHS Scotland, 2001). This political energy also created a four-year seconded post in Scottish government known colloquially as the Health and Homelessness Tsar, who then drove the implementation of the guidance in the form of NHS Board-level Health and Homelessness Action Plans and the creation of 'Health and homelessness standards' in 2005 (Scottish Executive, 2005). The then health minister gave personal and committed support to the implementation of the guidance and would personally call NHS territorial health boards to report on their Action Plans as part of his Annual Accountability Review process alongside other issues such as cancer treatment targets. This political support from the top was instrumental to the attention given by the NHS to the health needs of the homeless. However, soon after the publication of the six standards against which health boards were expected to 'self-assess', the Scottish government Health and Homelessness Tsar secondment ended and the intention was for the reporting mechanism to become mainstreamed. As predicted by some, this did not happen as, with no clear scrutiny and accountability of the self-reporting mechanism, interest in the standards waned and the

healthcare needs of the homeless slipped down and, for some Boards, off the agenda. It was only as a result of a question posed from a conference floor to another health minister some years later about this 'commitment drift' that led, in response by the minister, to the recreation of a group to look once again at the issue of the health of Scotland's homeless population. This national group was called the Health and Homelessness Group (Scottish Government, n.d.), which over time and led by NHS Health Scotland began the movement that has brought a resurgence of attention to homeless health and well-being. With hindsight the lesson is clear – the plight of the homeless in society requires robust, sustained and courageous political support by MSPs and relevant ministers plus annual scrutiny of territorial health board and local authority actions across the country.

The power of partnerships and public health persuasion

In 2015 a report commissioned by the Scottish Directors of Public Health and duly published by the ScotPHN became a catalyst for an energetic public health engagement with housing and homelessness providers at national and local level. Entitled 'Restoring the public health response to homelessness in Scotland' (Hetherington and Hamlet, 2015), it drew attention to the leadership role for public health in drawing partner agencies together to jointly act in preventative and responsive approaches. In addition, it shone a light on the shocking health of those experiencing homelessness and provided an opportunity for various sectors to come together to gain a common understanding of the routes into homelessness and to develop actions for policy and practice to both prevent and mitigate the impacts of homelessness.

Homelessness was presented as:

> Both a consequence and a cause of poverty, social and health inequality. It is also, in many cases, a late marker of severe and complex disadvantage which can be identified across the life course of individuals (Hetherington and Hamlet, 2015, p. 4).

And building on the human rights and inequity aspects of homelessness: 'The issue of homelessness prevention is a good downstream marker of attention to poverty and the socioeconomic determinants of health' (Hetherington and Hamlet, 2015, p. 5).

As will be expanded in a later chapter, the report shone a light on the critical issue of early childhood experiences: 'Early childhood trauma can often lie at the root of multiple exclusion homelessness highlighting the need to recognise this as an early sign' (Hetherington and Hamlet, 2015, p. 10).

In the same year the Commission on Housing and Wellbeing – a blueprint for Scotland's future – was published (Commission on Housing and Wellbeing, 2015). This work initiated by Shelter Scotland framed wellbeing across eight domains and gave added impetus for the housing sector to rightly position housing policy and delivery at the centre of population well-being while calling for greater action by NHS and the newly formed HSCPs.

The power of data linkage

In June 2018 the Scottish government, through the National Records of Scotland, released the first ever country study into the relationship between health and homelessness (Waugh et al., 2018). This report spans fifteen years of data and compares a cohort of almost 438,000 individuals assessed as homeless with age-sex matched controls resident in the 20% least deprived areas and the 20% most deprived areas of Scotland. In all a total of 1.3 million individuals were included in the study, which examined their healthcare utilisation across six NHS Scotland datasets together with information about any deaths from the National Records of Scotland. The results are compelling and provide the strongest evidence yet in Scotland for the need to comprehensively address the stark health inequalities arising in association with the experience of homelessness.

Homelessness legislation and implementation in Scotland since 2016

Scottish government has always prided itself on the progressive nature of its homelessness legislation and states that: 'Scotland has among the strongest rights in Europe for people facing homelessness. Reducing homelessness is a vital part of tackling poverty' (Scottish Government, 2016c). Under the Housing (Scotland) Act 1987, as amended, a person should be treated as homeless, even if they have accommodation, if it would not be reasonable for them to continue to stay in it. All local authorities have a legal duty to help people who are homeless or at risk of becoming homeless. They do this by providing information and advice and by offering temporary or permanent accommodation if circumstances warrant it. Since the abolition of priority need in 2012, everyone who is accepted as unintentionally home-less has the right to settled accommodation. The Housing (Scotland) Act 2001 requires local authorities to provide information and advice to enquirers on the prevention of homelessness and on services available to the homeless person. Further guidance was issued as the 'Code of guid-ance on homelessness' (Scottish Government, 2005) and the 'Prevention of homelessness guidance' (Scottish Government, 2009). A summary of current legislation in Scotland and the differences across the four devolved nations is available within the annual Scottish statistical report (Scottish Government, 2018d).

The Housing (Scotland) Act 2010 reinforced the call on local authori-ties to assess the housing support needs of homeless applicants, and this was to be delivered with a more preventative and early intervention focus leading to further Housing Options Guidance (Scottish Government, 2016b). This Housing Options approach is described thusly: 'a person-centred and preventative approach which looks at an individual's options and choices in the widest sense. This approach features early interven-tion and explores all possible tenure options'.

The 'Housing advice note' (Scottish Government, 2015) was significant in clarifying the statutory guidance to the newly formed HSCPs, health boards and local authorities on their joint responsibilities to involve hous-ing services in the integration of health and social care. The Public Bodies (Joint Working) (Scotland) Act 2014 regulations prescribe the housing-related functions that *must* be delegated by a local authority to the HSCP and those housing-related functions that *may* be delegated subject to local agreement. Unfortunately, 'functions in relation to homelessness' lie in the 'may be' list, thus across Scotland there is a postcode lottery as to which HSCPs have accepted homelessness functions under the above Acts. Yet the partnership working between housing, health and associated services such as adult and community justice social work, drug and alcohol services and community mental health teams is a key driver for the effective deliv-ery of practical support to the homeless community. The nature of these very varied partnership arrangements are described in the HSCP's housing contribution statements (Scottish Government, 2015), which must cover key areas such as adaptations, housing support and homelessness and the housing contribution across groups including older people and those with disabilities, mental health and addictions.

Much Scottish government attention has been paid to rough sleeping and homelessness over the past two years, culminating in the twenty-nine recommendation of the Homeless and Rough Sleeping Action Group (Scottish Government, 2017) and the outcome of a Report on Homelessness by the Scottish government local government and communities committee in 2018 (Scottish Government, 2018a). The implementation of these recommendations is now being taken forward by a jointly chaired Scottish government and COSLA group called the Homelessness Prevention Strategy Group. In addition, the past two Scottish government's Annual Programmes for Government documents have laid out definitive actions in relation to affordable housing and to the prevention and mitigation of rough sleeping and homelessness. In summary, there would appear to be consistent and high-level commitment within government to seriously address the causes and the consequences of Scottish homelessness.

Delivery of services

Political will and the will of the people are necessary drivers to sustain any step change in how a society views its homeless citizens. But delivery of individual outcomes for each homeless individual in city, market town or rural glen requires a matrix of agencies delivering services on the ground. Who delivers for the homeless in Scotland?

As stated earlier, the legal duty regarding the provision of accommodation and support lies with local authorities. Following the move towards the more preventative Housing Options approach and associated guidance (Scottish Government, 2016b), together with an increased engagement with third-sector commissioned services, councils are now being required to address their use of temporary accommodation with a focus on 'rapid re-housing' (Social Bite, 2017) as the norm. This includes the development of Housing First – the provision of ordinary settled housing as a first response for people with multiple and complex needs. The evidence base for Housing First is strong and Scotland now has its own national partnership known as Housing First Scotland and initial funding (Corra Foundation, 2018) to draw together best practice and monitor the rollout across local authorities. Local housing partnerships within each local authority area work with their local HSCPs and NHS Boards to ensure homelessness prevention is coordinated across the public services. The alignment of actions between housing, health and social care – and, in particular, the approach taken by individual HSCPs – will be critical for success.

In December 2017 the Scottish Prison Service (SPS) released Sustainable Housing On Release for Everyone (SHORE) standards (Scottish Prison Service, 2017). These are Scottish quality standards for housing advice, information and support for people in and leaving prison. The standards reflect the individual's journey namely:

- on imprisonment (including remand);
- during imprisonment;
- prior to release;
- following imprisonment.

Plans are in place to extend these standards with two additional stages:

- on arrest;
- at court.

These standards are seen as a service exemplar, and the Homelessness Prevention Strategy Group (HPSG) would like to see such service standards developed for other institutions. The SPS employs throughcare support officers in each establishment, who will work with individuals in preparation for release, on release and for up to twelve weeks post release.

The contribution of the third sector cannot be underestimated. Although operating under tight commissioning arrangements, these charities and social enterprises mostly deliver highly personalised and flexible support and accommodation at local, regional and national levels. Partnerships and networks across services exist in the major cities, while national networks such Homeless Action Scotland (HAS) and Glasgow Homeless Network (GHN) provide forums for sharing knowledge and best practice. A national model for empowered street outreach underpinned by shared training and trauma-informed practice is in preparation following the success of winter initiatives in 2017/18 in Scotland's four major cities.

Churches and other faith communities are known for their long-standing commitment to the homeless and rough sleeping community. Larger agencies such as the Salvation Army, Bethany Christian Trust and Glasgow City Mission are fully integrated into local partnership arrangements and are seen as valued partners in local planning of services such as winter shelters.

While the above list is by no means exhaustive, it demonstrates the multi-professional spectrum of agencies which together deliver the frontline service for the homeless community. But more exciting is the manner in which these services are evolving and engaging with the growing evidence around the drivers of MEH and the personal stories of those with lived experience.

The landscape of tomorrow

Scotland is poised for significant progress in its emerging vision for the elimination of homelessness, the eradication of rough sleeping and a societal shift in attitudes and responses. There is a momentum of political will evidenced across two consecutive 'programmes for government', a significant expansion of the government's civil servant policy team, an agreed funding stream and a much energised multi-partner, high-level group known as the Homelessness Prevention Strategy Group (Scottish Government, 2018e). Jointly chaired by the Minister for Local Government, Housing and Planning and the COSLA community well-being spokesperson, this group is responsible for the delivery of actions arising from the Homeless and Rough Sleepers Action Group (HARSAG)(Scottish Government, 2018a) recommendations referred to earlier. Actions will focus around:

- eradication of rough sleeping;
- transforming the use of temporary accommodation;
- ending homelessness.

Changes to frontline services including street outreach with a stronger trauma-informed workforce empowered to hold personal budgets are in process. Underpinning this national model will be a national academy providing training and support. There is growing awareness of the evidence base surrounding ACEs and their association with a number of the common risk factors for homelessness. This knowledge linked to the critical importance of psychologically informed practice and commissioning will be discussed in a later chapter. Regarding temporary accommodation, all local authorities are to draw up plans on how they intend to reduce the use of temporary accommodation and adopt a rapid rehousing approach by default with a Housing First model for those with multiple and complex disadvantage. In addition to driving for changes to the UK welfare arrangements, there will be a revision of legislation surrounding local connection and intentionality, and the current statutory code of guidance is to be updated. The current Housing Options approach will be further developed into Personal Housing Plans (PHPs). Lastly is a drive for improvements to homelessness data collection including a mechanism to enumerate rough sleeping in Scotland and to include both homelessness and housing data into a comprehensive dashboard of administrative health and social care datasets to be made available to managers in NHS Boards and HSCPs as a data-sharing tool (known as SHARE) (ISD Scotland, 2018) for comprehensive health and social care integration. The recent creation of a Housing First Scotland network and the emerging evidence gathering and synthesis work of the Centre for Homelessness Innovation (CHI) add additional resources to Scotland's attention to societal homelessness. Add to this, the impact of Josh Littlejohn, a socially minded entrepreneur who has established a chain of homelessness-focused sandwich bars called Social Bite and who organises annual high-profile winter Big Sleep Outs to raise awareness and funding for Housing First pilots across the four major cities in Scotland.

Conclusion

In the early years following devolution, Scotland entered a phase to decisively act in response to homelessness and ensure the healthcare system partnered in the work through the publication of the Scottish Health and Homelessness Standards in 2005 (Scottish Executive, 2005). In the decade that followed, these standards slowly slipped from the attention of NHS Boards. But now there has been a resurgence of attention to the health and social plight of those experiencing homelessness, as well as a new landscape of public and third-sector partnerships working to address the underlying causes and consequences – many of which have devastating impacts on health expectancy and quality of life. Public health has an enduring part to play in this endeavour.

CHAPTER 6

Pathways into and out of Homelessness: Lessons to be learnt

The experience of homelessness has a profound impact on health and well-being, and 'solutions' to homelessness circulate around finding both a house (a place of physical shelter) and a home (a place of belonging in the world). This chapter will highlight the research-based evidence that supports explanations of pathways into MEH and then draw on available research-based evidence to suggest ways that health and well-being can be improved for those who live in the most marginal spaces in society. Understanding that there are no easy 'solutions', an intersectional approach will be taken to engage with the complexities of diverse lives.

Since the 1970s, there has been increasing interest by government agencies, charities, researchers and politicians in solving homelessness. Each perspective has sought to identify, define and 'solve' homelessness, while imbuing the term, and the social category, with moral, social and political significance (McDonald and Marston, 2005). In particular, this has focused on people who live at the most extreme end of homelessness, such as those sleeping on the streets and those who experience MEH. In a recent large-scale review of the international literature, Mackie *et al.* (2017) suggest five different approaches to end rough sleeping: recognise the heterogeneity of local housing and support needs; take urgent action to find emergency shelter; use assertive outreach services; put Housing First in action; and make sure that services are person-centred. In addition to emphasising the requirement for immediate emergency accommodation to provide shelter from the elements, much of this report centres on the necessity of additional support services for people who experience MEH, not merely housing provision alone. For people who have experienced MEH, emergency hostels should provide only a temporary shelter and people should be moved into more appropriate housing with the support services as soon as possible.

Reeve *et al.* (2007) suggested homelessness as a 'career' but, in subsequent years, routes in, and out, of homelessness have been identified and conceptualised in different ways (Johnson *et al.*, 2015). In recent years, the 'pathway' metaphor has been developed further by a range of different scholars (Chamberlain and Johnson, 2013; Fitzpatrick *et al.*, 2013; Morris *et al.*, 2005; Piat *et al.*, 2015; Tutty *et al.*, 2013). As increasing numbers of people find themselves experiencing homelessness and subsequent deteriorating health, there have been increasing efforts to identify the ways that people 'enter' and 'exit' homelessness and, in doing so, to be able to prevent and intervene at points in the 'pathway' where people are most exposed to risk and vulnerability.

The focus of much of this work has been around MEH (Carter, 2007; Fitzpatrick *et al.*, 2011b) and rough sleeping. In a quantitative study of MEH in seven cities in the UK, Fitzpatrick *et al.* (2012) found fairly consistent pathways into homelessness across all of the cities. MEH was strongly linked to experiences of 'deep exclusion' such as childhood trauma and mental ill health and substance misuse early in life. The same study also highlighted the overlap between substance misuse, institutional care (prison, local authority care or hospital), begging, street drinking and homelessness (Fitzpatrick *et al.*, 2011a). Qualitative studies have likewise identified substance abuse, relationship breakdown and mental ill health as strong individual factors into street homelessness in Canada (Piat *et al.*, 2015). In addition, this study also highlighted structural insecurity in the transitions between young people in looked-after care and settled housing in the community as a pathway into homelessness. While a 'pathway' approach might suggest a linear trajectory, these authors acknowledge the complexity of homelessness and the multiple ways that these 'pathways' all intersect with each other. For example, it is well established that prisoners have been exposed to high levels of ACEs, violence and mental ill health and that the prison environment itself can be detrimental to mental health. More than 40% of people in prison suffer from mental ill health (Schneider, 2007), and prisoners have alarmingly high all-cause mortality and mortality from injuries and poisonings (Aldridge *et al.*, 2017).

Improving health and well-being

While the focus of this book has been to situate the experience of homelessness as 'ordinary' within the wider context of global health inequalities, healthcare discourse remains stubbornly rooted in behavioural causes of homelessness as 'extraordinary', particularly in relation to mental ill health and harmful substance use. The focus of this approach is in finding 'solutions' to improve the healthcare needs of those who sleep rough, engage in harmful substance use, are the victims and perpetrators of violence and experience poor mental ill health. While a recent review in the *Lancet* (Luchenski *et al.*, 2017) identifies a range of different health interventions that work in inclusion health, the focus of health service provision is primarily directed towards people who sleep rough and is three pronged: getting people off the streets; treating people on the streets; and preventing people ending up on the streets. While controversial because of the relatively small numbers of people in the population, people who sleep rough experience complex and multiple needs, are more difficult to house, are more in contact with the criminal justice system and use a disproportionately high cost of service provision in many countries – Canada, USA and Europe (Chambers *et al.*, 2013; Culhane *et al.*, 2011; Gaetz *et al.*, 2013). The healthcare literature alternatingly refers to these people as 'vulnerable' or 'chaotic'. In addition to poor health outcomes, people experiencing 'deep exclusion' (Dwyer and Somerville, 2011) incur high health costs to the public purse as substance use and mental ill health are driven by several factors including increased hospital admissions and increased use of the criminal justice system (Zaretzky *et al.*, 2017).

There is little doubt now that homelessness and harmful substance use are closely associated, both influencing the other (Pleace, 2008), and people who are homeless and/or experience mental ill health use alcohol and/or drugs to 'self-medicate' to manage mental distress and the hardships of life on the streets. Healthcare research has focused primarily on the associations between homelessness, harmful substance use and mental ill health and mental illness is a bi-directional 'risk-factor' for homelessness (Shelton *et al.*, 2009). Increasingly, researchers exploring the relationship between ACEs and childhood trauma assert that harmful substance use in childhood is a strong driver into homelessness in later life (Fitzpatrick *et al.*, 2013). People with long-term and severe mental ill health are likely to experience extended and repeated periods of rough sleeping (Goering *et al.*, 2011; Padgett *et al.*, 2006). Canadian researchers found a high prevalence of harmful substance use and mental ill health in people experiencing homelessness

(Aubry *et al.*, 2015), and similar results have been found in England (St Mungo's, 2013), the USA and Australia (Fazel *et al.*, 2014).

Harmful drug use and homelessness are of particular concern in Scotland: drug-related deaths in Scotland in 2017 were the highest recorded in Europe – being up 8% compared to 2016. This has been termed in the media as a 'public health emergency' (Cramb, 2018). Of the 61,000 estimated drug addicts in Scotland, there were 934 deaths recorded as a direct result of drug overdose, and 70% of these were in the over thirty-fives. These drug-related death rates are two-and-a-half times higher than in the rest of the UK. The deaths appear to be mainly in the older, long-term users, and heroin and methadone were implicated in the majority of deaths (87%), although cocaine, sedatives and the new synthetic psychoactive drugs were also recorded. Greater Glasgow and Clyde accounted for 30% of the recorded deaths (National Records of Scotland, 2018). As I write, the Scottish National Party (SNP) Scottish government is formulating a new drug and alcohol treatment strategy, due to be released in autumn 2018.

Injecting drug users are at particular risk of multiple adverse health outcomes and have a poor quality of life. The Edinburgh Addiction Cohort study is longitudinal research started in 1980 that has followed injecting drug users from one GP practice in Edinburgh over time. The researchers reported in 2010 that 50% of those who started injecting in late adolescence were dead by middle age (Macleod *et al.*, 2010). In 2010, the Scottish government implemented the Scottish naloxone programme, which aimed to reduce drug-related deaths (McAuley *et al.*, 2012), and the same study team found that there were definite benefits of opioid substitution delivered in primary care over time. Other studies have suggested that these benefits are due to improved social relationships and the subsequent reduction in criminal activity and healthcare attendance (Department of Health *et al.*, 2007). Moving from drug injecting to methadone also reduces the risk of blood-borne viruses associated with injecting, such as hepatitis C, and people who are homeless are at higher risk of HIV, TB and hepatitis C (Asten *et al.*, 2004). Beijer *et al.* (2012) carried out a systematic review of the international literature (USA, Europe and Japan) and found a range of prevalence rates. For TB, prevalence rates ranged from 0.2% to 7.7%; for hepatitis C from 3.9% to 36.2% and for HIV from 0.3% to 21.1%. The authors conclude that it is very difficult to accurately compare studies across countries because of the heterogeneity of the population under study and differences in definitions of homelessness. With recent HIV outbreaks in Glasgow and persisting HIV levels in Edinburgh, homelessness remains an enduring problem (Robertson, 2017).

Although it is clear that health and social care practitioners struggle to find 'solutions' to harmful substance use, there are innovative policies and practice in Scotland and further afield. After a long and protracted battle with the alcohol industry, the Scottish Parliament passed the law on minimum unit pricing in 2018 (Scottish Government, 2018b), which increased the cost of the cheapest cider and alcoholic drinks. The impact of this is too early to know, but it is hoped that this will reduce alcohol consumption. A range of research studies are focusing on harm-reduction measures as diverse as brief alcohol interventions in prisons (Shorter *et al.*, 2017) and using photographic methodologies to explore notions of recovery (Shortt *et al.*, 2017). In both research and healthcare interventions, the participation of experts by experience is seen as vital in shaping the design and delivery of interventions (Abdulkadir *et al.*, 2016).

In the Canadian context, Pauly (2014) describes the success of nurse-led clinics to foster trust and diminish stigma for people experiencing harmful substance use and discrimination. Harm-reduction models are increasingly being used to mitigate the negative consequences of substance use, and examples include Ottawa Inner City, which is a unique model of providing healthcare to people who experience homelessness with complex needs. In a residential setting, clients are given regulated amounts of alcohol each day in an attempt to control their alcohol consumption and to improve health (Farrell et al., 2014).

Treating people on the streets: Outreach services

People who live with homelessness have a high utilisation of hospital emergency services, particularly emergency services, and primary care is widely recognised as the most appropriate and effective setting to treat healthcare needs (Starfield, 2012). Nonetheless, people categorised as MEH often have reduced access to primary care, and barriers to accessing healthcare services include negative staff attitudes and stigma (Hwang and Burns, 2014; Kertesz *et al.*, 2014, inflexibility of services (Anderson *et al.*, 2006) and the challenges of treating people with complex needs (Crane *et al.*,

2011). In addition, migrants are often unaware of how health care services are accessed (Redman *et al.*, 2011). Specialist services for people who identify as homelessness are organised, led and implemented in different countries in a variety of ways, ranging from nurse-led clinics in inner-cities (Hewett *et al.* 2012), to 'walk-in' medical centres, to GP practices providing enhanced or targeted services, to outreach teams providing healthcare in hostels or day centres. In-reach services, where primary care teams go into hospitals and are involved in discharge planning, have been shown to have positive outcomes for people experiencing homelessness (Hewett *et al.*, 2016). Nonetheless, outreach services in the homelessness sector can be fragmented, even working against each other, as organisations jostle for funding, space and distinction in the services they offer (Smith and Hall, 2018).

There has been a concerted effort in recent years to help to better engage people who experience homelessness with health services, and assertive outreach has been demonstrated to be a positive approach in a range of different contexts (Blackburn *et al.*, 2017). In a comparative study of an integrated team approach in Sacramento, USA, a team comprising a physician, nurses and social workers made weekly visits to transitional housing to offer HIV, TB and immunisation clinics. After eighteen months, the evaluation demonstrated reduced visits to the Emergency Department and increased uptake of screening services (Ciaranello *et al.*, 2006). Similar outcomes have been noted with integrated outreach services with chronic disease management (O'Toole *et al.*, 2010), HIV (Rosenblum *et al.*, 2006 and adherence to medication (Roche *et al.*, 2018. Developing trust, breaking down barriers to healthcare access and a collaborative approach between outreach services and primary healthcare clinics are key factors to success (Canavan *et al.*, 2012; Hwang and Burns, 2014). In addition, Canadian researchers assert that, as community and shelter-based health services are becoming the main way to improve health and well-being for people experiencing homelessness, the setting and design are crucial to engagement (McNeil and Guirguis-Younger, 2014).

Keeping people off the streets: Intermediate care

Intermediate care – the support to improve health and care following discharge, primarily from hospital – has been increasing in the UK since 2001. It is designed and delivered in different ways, but it has been largely pioneered by the Pathway charity (Pathway, 2017) and adopted in different ways throughout the country. Intermediate care was given a government funding boost in 2013, when the Department of Health launched a £10 million 'Homeless Hospital Discharge Fund'. This was largely triggered by a report from the third sector stating that more than 70% of people discharged from hospital in London find themselves back on the streets without adequate provision to meet their needs (Homeless Link and St Mungo's, 2012). In addition, continued funding is an ongoing challenge (Homeless Link, 2014). The purpose of the funding was to develop partnerships between the third sector, NHS and local government to improve hospital discharge for people at risk of homelessness; and fifty-two different projects were set in place. Cornes *et al.* (2018) carried out a realist synthesis of the intermediate care literature and found that intermediate care is a positive approach to reducing homelessness and improving healthcare outcomes for people experiencing homelessness, and they highlight the importance of integrated care planning and collaborative working. In addition, the authors note the importance of trauma-informed environments and that patients should be part of the care planning, not 'handed over' from one service to the other.

Finding people a permanent home: Housing First
Increasingly, it is recognised that, to treat mental ill health and harmful substance use, harm-reduction approaches alone are not enough. Housing and treatment are inextricably linked, and when provided in combination they are shown to have a positive impact on improving health and well-being (Briggs *et al.,* 2009; Tsemberis *et al.,* 2004; Wolitski *et al.,* 2010). For example, Marshall and Kerr (2015) report on an innovative and positively evaluated programme in Vancouver, Canada – the Dr Peter Centre (Krusi *et al.,* 2009). This is described as an integrated, assisted-living residential programme for HIV intravenous drug users and includes injecting and non-injecting drug rooms on site.

Housing First programmes have emerged in recent years as a key initiative in preventing long-term homelessness. Over the last decade, they have been rapidly implemented in many European and North American contexts and hailed as a 'revolutionary' approach by many (Busch-Geertsema, 2013). The programme has been implemented widely across the USA, Canada and in many Europeans countries and has been cautiously welcomed in the UK; however, many UK service providers do not perceive it to be a significant departure from existing serivce provision (Johnsen and Teixeira, 2012). A recent systematic review of Housing First (Woodhall-Melnik *et al.*, 2017) found that there is robust evidence that Housing First is successful in increasing housing retention and reducing homelessness in the USA. In addition, the authors found that Housing First also reduces the use of the criminal justice service and emergency health services. Further research is needed to robustly evaluate Housing First in other welfare contexts, such as Europe, Canada and Australia, but these findings reinforce the need for structural approaches to ensure that people with a history of long-term mental illness and substance use can begin treatment within a stable housing framework.

The premise of Housing First is that people are provided with suitable housing without a prerequisite of treatment compliance. The Housing First model was first developed in New York City by psychologist and founder of the Pathways to Housing organisation, Dr Tsemberis, as an alternative approach to the more usual 'treatment first' approach (Tsemberis and Eisenberg, 2000). While the 'treatment first' approach is dependent on evidence of successful treatment of mental illness or long-term substance use before independent tenancies are given to people who are long-term homeless, the Housing First approach prioritises tenancy housing as a *prerequisite* to treatment.

Typically, in the 'treatment first' approach, transitional housing is only provided on the basis that people are receiving treatment for mental ill health and/or substance use. Based on a 'step-up' approach, people are able to 'move up' to tenancies only if they are mentally stable and responding to treatment for substance use (Kertesz *et al.*, 2009; Pearson *et al.*, 2009). Being assessed as 'housing ready' is a standard that people need to attain if they are to be offered a housing tenancy. Concern has also been expressed that 'treatment first' approaches strip people of their rights to self-determination and control over the decisions they make in terms of housing and treatment (Kertesz *et al.*, 2009), and housing becomes something to be earned rather than a basic human right (Padgett *et al.*, 2006).

In contrast to this linear approach, the underlying philosophy of Housing First is that housing is a fundamental human right and not something that should be a 'reward' for treatment compliance (Tsemberis, 2010). While the Housing First approach devised in New York City has been shown to both reduce 'rough sleeping' (Padgett *et al.*, 2006, Padgett *et al.*, 2011) and increase the length of time people are retained in tenancies, especially those who have traditionally been hard-to-house (Woodhall-Melnik *et al.*, 2017), there is concern that the model has been implemented in other cultures and contexts without adhering to the original underlying philosophy of care.

As Housing First has proliferated in the Global North as a policy approach to ending long-term homelessness, the evaluation of different programmes in varying contexts has been problematic. Woodhall-Melnik and Dunn's (2015) systematic review primarily looked at the research-based evidence in the context of homeless services in the USA and concluded that Housing First increases time in tenancies, reduces involvement in the criminal justice system and emergency hospital attendance, and exhibits significantly higher improvements in quality of life for people who are experiencing homelessness. The research on drug and alcohol use has produced mixed results, and the authors call on more research to investigate the outcomes of Housing First on diverse populations.

While the central tenets of the original Pathways approach has been adopted in many countries, there are variations in the implementation in different local contexts. In the evaluation of the Housing First Europe project across five cities (Amsterdam, Budapest, Glasgow, Copenhagen and Lisbon), Busch-Geertsema (2013) states argues that Housing First models have largely adhered to the underlying philosophy of the pioneer Pathway model and yet points out that there is a tendency for programme drift when transferring the approach to different local contexts.

The positive results of the Housing First model have triggered a positive response from policymakers and governments around the world, including Scotland, as outlined in Chapter 5. Nonetheless, having a 'roof over one's head' is not the whole story: home is more than just a physical shelter but a feeling of safety, security and psychological well-being. Home is both a reality and an ideal and can be a therapeutic space in a confusing world to enable people to repair their identity, self-esteem and assist with recovery. Retention and performance indicators do not fully capture the lived experience of people who have experienced homelessness, and research exploring the meanings of 'home' has proliferated over the last two decades.

The meaning of home: Mental health, ontological security and well-being

Scholars, practitioners and policymakers all realise that it is a long distance travelled between sleeping rough and having a home: a home is somewhere that is idealised, imbued with meaning and so much more than merely a roof over your head. To have a home acknowledges the importance of the physical, legal and social boundaries of home for health and well-being. The conceptualisation of home is much more than a structural shelter, and sociology scholars invite us to more fully understand the importance of home as an entity that is used to express identity, maintain mental health and ensure well-being.

Somerville (1992) was one of the first theorists to explore the multiple meanings of 'home' for those who are homeless. In contrasting 'roofless-ness' with 'homelessness', he identified the elements of home as: 'shelter, hearth, privacy, roots, abode and (possibly) paradise' (Somerville, 1992, p. 332). This builds on early optimistic and idealised notions of home as a place of privacy, identity, safety, family and belonging (Saunders and Williams, 1988). While it is widely recognised as a place of physical shelter, of social relationships and of idealised associations, it is also a place of contested identities and porous boundaries. Home is a place imbued with meaning (Mallett, 2004) and a place where identity is shaped and children are nurtured (Saunders and Williams, 1988). A wide range of scholars have identified the mental health benefits of home (Kidd and Evans, 2010; Ahmet, 2013; Alaazi et al., 2015), and safety, security, privacy and control are key components of this. Home is a place where it is possible to escape the pressures of a fluid world and to be private, secure and safely hidden against the pressures of the public world.

Sociologist Anthony Giddens first conceptualised this sense of 'being in the world' (Giddens, 1991, p. 92) as ontological security and argues that ontological security is established in childhood and is an emotional need in all societies. Certainly, many scholars see the importance of ontological security for people who are experiencing mental illness (Laing, 1965; Padgett, 2007), for homeless women (Tomas and Dittmar, 1995), indigenous people (Alaazi et al., 2015) and those living in conflict zones (Sousa et al., 2014). It is clear that having a sense of home is important to emotional health and well-being, beyond merely having a roof over one's head. Dupuis and Thorns (1998) argue that:

much of the work that goes into maintaining or restoring a sense of ontological security takes place in the private realm, where tensions built up from the constant surveillance in other settings of daily life can be relieved (Dupuis and Thorns, 1998, p. 27).

The idea of ontological security has emerged as an important psychological concept, and this seems to be important for people who are experiencing homelessness, as well as for people who are housed. Nonetheless, for many people who are housed in B&Bs, hostels, temporary and overcrowded accommodation, there is little sense of ontological security and little relief from the tensions of daily life (Mackie *et al.*, 2017). Research repeatedly highlights the experience of people in shelters who feel like their lives are under surveillance – rules of entry dominate these accounts – and B&B accommodation is often shaped by strict curfew. Safety, security, privacy and control can be absent in these environments, and accounts of people living in these types of accommodation are imbued with frustrations that others are watching their comings-and-goings, fears of physical and psychological danger, exit and entry regulations, the prohibition of pets in the premises and descriptions of a dwelling that is far from the notion of a home.

Notions of home are complex and far from being a simple ideal; many people negotiate a complex interplay of safety and danger within the home. Sousa *et al.* (2014) uncovers the ways that women protect ontological security during house raids by Israeli forces in Palestine, and a significant amount of research with women who experience domestic abuse has uncovered the complex ways that women simultaneously manage ontological security in the home for their children, while living with a dangerous partner. For people who experience gender-based violence, the home can clearly be a site that simultaneously offers privacy and safety from the streets, but also harbours danger and violence within the walls (Woodhall-Melnik *et al.*, 2017). Yet, for many others who experience homelessness, studies show that they would rather sleep on the streets than stay in the bricks-and-mortar accommodation they have been given as they experience social isolation and loneliness. Living on the streets can bring a sense of community, companionship, friendship and feelings of 'home' that are lacking in isolated flats on the edges of cities. In Ravenhill's (2014) ethnographic doctoral study of homelessness, she contends that homelessness culture operates as a counterculture and brings a sense of belonging and identity. Likewise, in research in Stoke-on-Trent, Brown *et al.* (2008) used a 'life story' approach (McAdams, 1993) to interview people about their experiences of homelessness and found that hostels and the streets were a valuable source of social networks, friendship and support. In Watkin's (2013) fascinating ethnography with people who live in vans in California, the quasi-private space of the van was an important aspect of recreational vehicle (RV) living, including the social networks built up by vehicle living. This work supports the findings of Hyde (2005), who found that the strength of social relationships are important factors in shaping the decision of people to exit homelessness. In addition, research in Australia demonstrated that street relationships can also encourage a deepening entrenchment into rough sleeping and can develop a camaraderie that is difficult to leave behind (Johnson and Chamberlain, 2008).

Although the idea of home has been explored substantially within the context of a range of different groups and measures, research on 'home' with people experiencing homelessness has only recently been explored. Padgett's (2007) qualitative study in the USA was one of the first to highlight the importance of ontological security for people who were homeless and experiencing severe mental illness. Woodhall-Melnik *et al.* (2017) found that homeless men in a Canadian context used concepts such as comfort, safety and independence to describe housing stability, rather than the material markers of housing stability used by policymakers such as permanence, adequacy and affordability (Pearson *et al.*, 2009).

Lived experience: David

David, a thirty-two-year-old Scottish man, had lived between the prison system, B&B accommodation and hostels for much of his adult life when he eventually was able to maintain a secure tenancy. In a qualitative research study in 2017 exploring GP outreach services, David explained to me how difficult he was finding it to live alone. I met David at a crisis centre in Scotland in 2017 and he explained the reasons he was thinking of returning to hostel accommodation, even though he had a tenancy in a flat in a social housing estate on the edge of the city:

> 'I miss all of the guys, yeh ken. I really miss the guys in the hostel. You just gae back to the hoose noo and look at the walls. It's awful. I dinnae ken how long I'm gonnae last. I hate it. It was better before. In the hostel. I miss thae guys'.

A sense of ontological security is particularly problematic for forced migrants, searching for cultural identity and a new home within a new country and culture. This is compounded when they become homeless and lose a cultural sense of home, as well as physical shelter. Having already experienced torture, loss of close family members, bereavement and severe psychological trauma in their home country, many forced migrants struggle with mental ill health as they become destitute and search for a sense of self, identity and home in a new land. It is common for people who have become homeless following the asylum process in the UK to describe the asylum system itself as a form of mental torture, especially when their experiences of torture, war, persecution, escape and survival are not believed.

Lived experience: Jamal

In research I carried out with people seeking asylum in the north-east of England in 2013, I clearly remember Jamal, an Algerian man, who vividly explained the mental strain of finding himself homeless in a foreign country such as the UK:

> 'There are some people who become crazy because of thinking too much about their situation [refusal and subsequent destitution], who have been in this situation for a long time and as I heard from other people, as I see by myself, I think we will become sick and tired when you think about all that has happened to you and what the Home Office said about you and not being believed.'

While the causes and consequences of health and homelessness are inextricably intertwined, finding a home away from the street is important for mental well-being, safety and security. Nonetheless, much of this research focuses on single male homelessness, and this can obscure the ways that different people experience homelessness, especially women, people who identify as LGBT and young people (Durso and Gates, 2012; Watson and Cuervo, 2017). The home has long been recognised as somewhere where gender relations are enacted, sustained and where identity is formed (Davis, 2001). Men and women understand home in different ways and, as such, understandings of the gendered experience of leaving home and becoming homeless are increasingly understood as a gendered construction. Bowpitt *et al.* (2011) assert that complex relationships of oppression and identity operate in the family home and that discourses constructing women's homelessness have been shaped as 'both an *escape* and an intensely felt source of *loss*' (Bowpitt *et al.*, 2011, p. 537; italics in original). In all of these different contexts, a sense of 'home' is an experience, an identity and part of complex gender relationships that accentuate the importance of 'home' as something different to merely having a house and worthy of consideraton in discussions of homelessness, health and well-being.

Homelessness and health as a gendered experience

There has been a predominance of studies exploring the experiences of men in relation to health outcomes, which is understandable as men make up 84–89% of people who sleep rough in England (Savage, 2009; Fitzpatrick *et al.*, 2018b). Although difficult to verify, these figures seem to be consistent with many countries in Europe and the USA. This has provoked comment that homeless women are rendered invisible in research and has renewed calls for increased research into the health and well-being of women who experience homelessness (Wolf *et al.*, 2016). Such invisibility is largely due to the understanding that housing policy puts women with dependent children as a priority housing need. In addition, women who flee gender-based violence are also positioned as 'vulnerable' and given priority housing.

There have been several studies that have challenged this idea. Reeve *et al.* (2006) found that 60% of their sample of people slept rough at some point but that women used public spaces in different ways to men and were less visible on the streets. Hutchinson *et al.* (2014) asserted that at least 30% of people using accommodation projects in London were women, and that women were subjected to sexual violence, bereavement, relationship breakdown and separation from children. May *et al.* (2007) built on Wardhaugh's (1999, cited in May *et al.*, 2007) theory of men 'colonising' the streets by taking on a tough man exterior and making their bodies visible on the streets, whereas women 'conceal' their bodies by becoming invisible. The authors extend this idea by arguing that British women in their research manage street sleeping in very different ways to men. The authors develop their own typology of the ways that women manage street homelessness: those who distanced themselves from homelessness identity; those who remained 'in the shadows of the street scene'; those who identified with the street homeless scene; and those who formed a different identity. This also makes women more invisible in 'rough sleeper' headcounts and under-represented in official statistics.

It has long been understood that gender-based violence has been a reason for homelessness for women. In a qualitative study comparing the experiences of 105 homeless men and women in the UK, Bowpitt *et al.* (2011) found that around 50% of both men and women had undergone a major trauma, high levels of violence and bereavement of a close relative. Three-quarters of people had lived with family breakdown and mental ill health, and nearly all men were harmful substance users. What was particularly interesting in this study was that men and women left the family home for different reasons: women because they were fleeing high levels of domestic abuse; men because they were walking away from complex family issues. There is a growing body of evidence that asserts that a number of women turn to sex work in order to avoid a life on the streets, particularly if they engage in harmful substance use; in contrast, men are more likely to engage in criminal activity (Bowpitt *et al.,* 2011). Domestic abuse experienced by migrant women is often obscured by concerns around immigration status, cultural norms and values and stigma (Ogunsiji *et al.,* 2012).

A growing body of research is emerging that uncovers the ways that women engage in survival sex in order to secure a roof over their heads (Reeve *et al.,* 2006). The majority of this work in the health field focuses on sex work and sexually transmitted infections. The health literature is predominantly based on a 'vulnerability' approach to sex work, whereas studies originating in the field of housing studies have demonstrated the ways that women are active in using survival sex strategies to reclaim a sense of control and identity after surviving earlier abuse and homelessness (McNoughton and Sanders, 2007) and make an active 'choice' to enter sex work (Harding and Hamilton, 2009). Watson (2011; 2016; 2017) has explored the ways that young women in Australia enter into intimate sexual relationships in order to protect themselves from the dangers of the street, even if those relationships are with violent men.

It is understood that young people experience homelessness in different ways to adults (Mallett *et al.,* 2010) and require different support and services. Measures to address youth homelessness must shift the conceptualisation of youth as high-risk runaways and engage in the complexities and subcultures of street life (Karabanow and Kidd, 2014). Nonetheless, the ways that the different intersections of gender and sexuality impact on understandings of homelessness is only recently being uncovered. In North America, studies suggest that LGBT youth make up 20–40% of young people living in homeless situations (Durso and Gates, 2012) and that they struggle with high levels of trauma, sexual abuse and difficulty in foster care (Ream and Forge, 2014). Disclosure of LGBT identity is an important factor in young people becoming homeless as they are 'kicked out' of the family home (Page, 2017). In the UK, this number is estimated at around 24% (Albert Kennedy Trust, 2015). Stigma and discrimination are high, with young homeless people reporting social exclusion in relation to their homeless status, sexuality and age (Mayberry, 2013). Compared to heterosexual young people, they are more likely to engage is harmful substance use and be victims of sexual abuse and use 'survival sex' as a strategy to manage life on the streets (Waft *et al.*, 2013). Ethnicity, age and structural barriers have also been shown to impact sexual health for young people who identify as homeless in a Canadian context (Schwartz *et al.*, 2014).

In order to end homelessness and thereby improve the health and well-being of the most excluded in our society, measures need to be implemented that take an intersectional approach to health and homelessness and to engage with the complexity of human experience, rather than on policies that focus predominantly on the ways that middle-aged white men sleeping in street doorways experience homelessness. In Scotland, there has been a renewed focus on prevention strategies and an unprecedented investment in health visiting services since 2015 to strengthen the workforce and to intervene in the early years and to prevent family stress and violence. This focus on support and intervention in the early years is in part in response to Marmot's (2010) European review of health inequalities and is seen as an important public health action. There has also been a strong focus on training and education of the healthcare workforce in identifying and intervening in domestic abuse, which has been introduced as a mandatory requirement of the new Health Visiting Universal Pathway introduced in Scotland in 2015.

Tackling stigma, discrimination, hate and racism also needs to have a renewed focus to prevent young LGBT people from being forced out of family homes and to enable refugees and people seeking asylum to find a sense of 'home' in a new land. In the healthcare arena, healthcare professionals should work with positive approaches to people experiencing homelessness, regardless of sexual orientation, country of origin or physical appearance. Much more could be done to enshrine anti-discriminatory practice in health and social care educational programmes.

Recognition of resilience should be built into health and social care discourse, where healthcare providers work to support the ways that people experiencing homelessness work to live and survive. Discourses of only vulnerability need to be challenged in ways that do not play into the neoliberal project of 'scroungers' or a 'threat within', and new narratives of homelessness, survival and resistance need to bring a more nuanced view of health, well-being and homelessness to the policy table. Policy changes can then support resilience, rather than punish the 'scroungers', and welfare benefits can be delivered in an equitable way to support health and well-being. The health and well-being of people experiencing homelessness will only be improved when health inequalities are tackled and social justice realised.

Conclusion

It is clear that 'pathways' into homelessness are varied and multidimensional and shaped by stigma, gender, age and sexuality, and these are contextualised within a neoliberal age. In order for effective 'solutions' to be achieved, policymakers, healthcare professionals and service providers need to engage with the nuances of the field and to take an intersectional approach in order to reduce homelessness and, in doing so, improve health and well-being.

CHAPTER 7

Relationships Matter: Psychologically informed approaches

Conversation with Adam Burley

After many years of focusing on housing and service provision, healthcare practitioners are increasingly understanding the value of relational aspects to health and social care. Psychologically informed approaches to healthcare delivery have gained traction in recent years, especially in the field of homelessness and health. This chapter presents a different format and is a piece 'in conversation' with Dr Adam Burley, a consultant clinical psychologist working with people experiencing homelessness in Edinburgh, who relates his personal experiences and perspective on working with people – and services – who experience trauma.

Current context

In Scotland, the focus has turned in recent years towards the complex trauma and violence suffered by children in their early years, and the impact this has on later life and the relationship this has to experiences of homelessness (Hutchinson *et al.,* 2014). While the concept is not new, and there is a plethora of research that has uncovered the relationship between abuse, trauma, injury and death in childhood and health and well-being (WHO, 2014), policy and research have adopted the terminology of ACEs to explore this in a wider context. In May 2016, the ScotPHN published a widely circulated report called *Polishing the Diamonds* (Coupar and Mackie, 2016) which conceptualised the children of Scotland as all potential diamonds by highlighting the fact that some children were never 'polished' with love, care, safety and security, and were, therefore, never able to reach their full potential or experience the best of health and well-being (Coupar and Mackie, 2016). First developed in the USA through a large study involving more than 17,000 people, the notion of ACEs has been accepted to mean: 'intrafamilial events or conditions causing chronic stress responses in the child's immediate environment. These include notions of maltreatment and deviation from societal norms' (Kelly-Irving *et al.*, 2013, p. 721).

The categorisation of ACEs is widely recognised as ten different experiences: emotional abuse; physical abuse; sexual abuse; emotional neglect; physical neglect; domestic violence; household substance misuse; household mental ill health; criminality; separation; and living in care. Whether poverty should be categorised as an ACE remains controversial. An increasing body of evidence in Wales, England and Scotland now demonstrates that the more ACEs someone experiences, the more likely they are to have been involved in violence, be a heroin/crack user, had an unplanned teenage pregnancy, be a smoker, been incarcerated at any point in their lifetime and be a binge drinker (Centre for Homelessness Impact, 2018). Increased rates of injury and death during childhood, premature mortality and suicide, disease and mental illness are all associated with ACEs (Institute of Health Equity, 2015).

In response to this, psychologically informed approaches to care are being developed and implemented in several centres across the UK (Breedvelt., 2016). Adam tells us of his experiences as a clinician in practice and of the importance of working in a psychologically informed way.

To begin, could you set the scene on relationships?

Choking up. Take a deep breath …

Breathing is essential for physical life. When going well it tends to run along in the backgrounds of our day-to-day lives, out of our attention, and, for the most part, in an unconscious fashion. With breathing it is not, perhaps, until we start choking that we begin to notice just how fundamental it is to our well-being. What was an automatic process that we had not given much consideration to suddenly becomes the sole focus of our attention, and the rising panic we feel tells us something about how utterly central to life this hitherto mundane process is.

In my experience, the same is true of our relationships. Human relationships are essential, providing the absolute fundament to our psychological, emotional and social functioning. Our brains and minds appear to run on relationships. They provide the medium through which we develop attachments and connections, that in turn allow us to do things such as develop friendships and families, raise children, play and create, secure occupation and broadly speaking connect with the social world. They underpin our emotional and psychological well-being; indeed, it may not be too much of a stretch to say that our mental health is our relationships, and vice versa. Similar to breathing, when relationships are going well they operate in the background, out of our consciousness and attention – a silent fabric underpinning all of our social existence. As I look around, I see that for those of us lucky enough to have relationships that run smoothly we are routinely oblivious to their subtlety and operation, and rarely find ourselves arriving home at the end of the day proudly reporting that we managed to relate really well all day! But just as with breathing, it is often only when our relationships 'choke' that we start to become aware of just how central to our lives these invisible processes are. We feel pain at a loss, sadness and worry when a friend tells us they no longer like us, and anxiety and distress when we feel we have been deeply misunderstood by another. We experience terrible fear when the life of our child or partner is at risk. When a relationship of value ends in whatever way, we may begin to feel its true importance through the emotional pain it leaves us with. From our earliest moments of relating to a primary caregiver in order to get our basic needs met to our last moments alive, it is the quality and nature of the interpersonal relationship world we inhabit that can begin to describe so much of our mental health and well-being.

As we can see in the lived experience of John, neglect and abuse in early life led to homelessness, harmful substance misuse and disengagement with services.

Lived experience: John

John is thirty-five-year-old man who was brought up in care from the age of five after it was recognised that his home environment was not physically or psychologically safe. He had experienced physical abuse and neglect by the time he went into care, and experienced further abuse while in care. As he aged he began to communicate his experiences through abusive behaviours towards those he perceived to be either a threat to him, or in a position of power. This included most people, and these interactions led to regular contact with the criminal justice services and periods of time in prison for violence-related crimes. He began rough sleeping, and using drugs and alcohol from around the age of sixteen, and continued to cycle in and out of homeless, health and criminal justice services for the rest of his teens and twenties. These relationships, like those he had in his personal life, seemed to oscillate between high demand of others, and aggressive rebuttals of any service that attempted to meet those demands. He would engage with services through not attending offered appointments, and then becoming angry when those services discharged him in response to his non-attendance. This meant that through the nineteen years that he had been known to services he had never managed to complete a single treatment regime, or remain in relationship with a service (outside of prison) for longer than three months. Relationships with housing and care providers would typically end in exclusion, discharge or eviction due to 'non-engagement'.

A psychological formulation described a severe ambivalence at the heart of understanding John's emotional and psychological needs. His demands for care were seen as a genuine request for assistance, while his rejection of care was viewed as being a defensive response to the anxiety that being in need of others evoked in him. This understanding was embedded in what was known about John's developmental history, and rather than seeing his non-attendance as non-engagement it was viewed as an extreme form of ambivalent attachment. John appeared to simultaneously be both desperate for help, and desperate to avoid it in equal measure.

While John was residing within a hostel that was attempting to develop a psychologically informed approach to care, this formulation was used to influence how the staff and service positioned themselves in relation to John. The informed plan was not complicated in nature, being organised around a simple approach of responding to John's ambivalent ways of relating by continuing to provide the opportunity for care past the point where mainstream services had typically pulled the plug. Support meetings were offered in a committed way *independent* of whether John attended or not, and importantly John's tenure in the accommodation was not contingent upon him engaging with support in a pre-determined way. Through this simple approach being provided consistently and coherently, and with staff support in place, John was able to sustain the supported accommodation for thirty-four months to date, attend support meetings on a regular basis, and begin to think about his future. This period of accommodation is the longest that John has ever been securely housed in his life, and the longest period he has ever gone without rough sleeping. He is able to report that there are members of staff that he trusts. Many of his difficulties remain, but it does feel as if he is starting to breathe a bit more easily.

It was only when John's accommodation was provided *independently* of his ability to manage healthy relationships that things turned around for him and he was able to sustain supported accommodation.

Through my work as a clinical psychologist, I see that, when many of our relationships are routinely problematic, we can find ourselves experiencing chronic psychological and emotional difficulties as a consequence. Taken to a logical endpoint, if all of our relationships were to choke badly, that is, if we were unable to maintain a single health-giving relationship, then we might quickly find ourselves becoming friendless, jobless, penniless, emotionally distraught and even homeless. If all of our relationships choked to the point where they ceased to exist then we might find ourselves detached, unknown and psychologically alone. When our breathing is seriously impaired there is a direct threat to our physical aliveness. Similarly, when our capacity to form and maintain relationships with other human beings is seriously impaired, there is a direct threat to our psychological and emotional aliveness.

I work daily with a group of people who are often referred to as the 'multiply excluded homeless', and I routinely hear stories of lives that begin in adversity and develop in circumstances where traumatic, neglectful and depriving experiences in relationships are commonplace. The people I work with report high levels of abuse, neglect and other forms of severe adversity and homelessness appears as a late emerging symptom in lives that have been marred by distressing and troubling relationships from the very outset. From this perspective, I see homelessness as just one symptom of a developmental pathway influenced by a range of known and predictable variables, rather than the random accident it is often portrayed to be. MEH does not just 'happen to anyone'.

How does extreme adversity impact the lives of the people you work with?

Extreme levels of adversity can have profound and long-lasting effects on the individuals who have experienced them. Over and above the plethora of neurological disturbances that trauma and neglect can have on the developing brain, the psychosocial consequences of developmental adversity can be devastating and hugely life limiting. In particular, childhood adversity can seriously impact upon an individual's developing sense of how they relate to others, and how others relate to them. This kind of history can give rise to serious disturbances in our capacity to form trusting and anxiety-free relationships with others, and so limit the degree to which an individual can develop both psychologically and emotionally. It can make intimacy and secure attachment difficult – if not impossible. As a consequence of these disturbances, the capacity of an individual to connect with the world and the people in it can be se verely damaged. In short, it can lead to a serious 'choking' in relationships, and at the severe end of the scale it can develop to the deep level of social exclusion that I so often see in this group. Severe adversity can give rise to deep ambivalence about interpersonal connection in an individual, it can progress to a person developing extremely disturbing ways of expressing their distress, and it can cause an extreme compromise in a person's capacity to do something as fundamental as trust another. These intra- and interpersonal responses to adversity and trauma are often at their most salient and alive when in relation to others, and can give rise to responses from the other that can often reflect the original adversity. Choking can kill – in relationships as in breathing.

All health and social care is fundamentally relational. It involves one group of people, often labelled as 'patients', 'service users' or 'clients', coming into contact with another group of people, often called things like 'support workers', 'doctors', 'social workers', 'psychologists' or 'nurses', in a relational dynamic that centres around the need for, and the provision of, care. Without taking notice of the relational elements of care when working with people from very adverse backgrounds, health and social care providers can often become caught up in the relational choking described above, and find themselves, with a greater or lesser degree of consciousness, re-enacting some of the neglecting, excluding and abusive behaviour.

One example of this can be seen in the way that health and social care services can often seem to relate to dependency. It would appear that many health and social care services are deeply phobic of dependency, and can spend a great deal of time and worry on 'fostering' dependency, and an almost equal amount trying to ensure that everyone they are in relation to moves towards 'independence'. Whether this is driven by the pragmatics of how services are funded, an unconscious fear of becoming attached to 'patients' and 'clients' or some other reason is unclear, but what does seem clearer to me is the unwritten rule that dependency is in some way bad, and not to be encouraged. I see this as most apparent in services that are organised around the dependent relationships that individuals have formed with non-humans, such as drug and alcohol services. Here the main task becomes organised around overtly trying to reduce an individual's dependency on one substance or another, while at the same time – typically more covertly – trying to ensure that the same person does not develop a dependency on the worker involved. It seems to me that this attempt to reduce one (drug) dependency while trying to ensure that another (human) one does not develop can cause difficulties for all involved. The person with a dependent relationship to a substance may remain deeply ambivalent about giving up their trusted relationship with the substance, while the worker becomes increasingly annoyed at the service-users failure to 'move on', 'progress' or in some other way 'get better'.

You talk a lot about dependency, can you explain this further?
In my experience, the dynamics within services seem to quietly forget that we are all utterly dependent. Indeed, it is our myriad deeply held dependencies to our partners, our children, our work and colleagues, to our record collections and football teams – not to mention our morning coffees and weekend drinks – that keep us psychologically and emotionally intact. For individuals who have experienced high levels of adversity, pain and trauma in their earliest experiences of human relationships, their first experiences of anxiety-reducing substances may be the first relationship they have had with anything that has made them feel calm, relaxed, contained and understood. It is easy to forget just how dependent we all were on others through the first years of our lives, and how addicted we were to the good that was provided to us during those times. Witness the healthy feeding baby, and their face of complete contentment and state of deep semi-conscious narcosis following a good feed. See how later on, when the effects wear off, they are to be found screaming for more, demanding further input of the thing that has made them feel so good. It is interesting how later on in life we can find ourselves calling these basic human processes things such as 'grouching', 'withdrawal' and 'challenging behaviour'. The individual who is afforded a healthy developmental experience in relation to caregivers who allow a dependency to develop, and are able to give enough to satisfy the psychological, physical and emotional demands of the individual, can grow and develop to a point where they may wean off this primary dependency, not into a state of independence (who is independent?), but into states of dependency that we call things such as family and friendships. For those

who, for whatever reason, did not receive enough, or for whom the receipt of anything from the other was run through with anxiety, uncertainty and pain, may be left doubly disadvantaged: firstly, in that their developmental psychological and emotional needs have not been met; and, secondly, that they have developed an understandable distrust, fear and ambivalence towards the objects where we typically get those needs met, that is, from other human beings.

The first experience of alcohol or heroin may give that person an experience that they have been deprived of to that point: it may make them feel good, contained, safe even. Over time it may become something that they can trust, something that they can rely on, something they can get into a relationship with to get their previously deprived needs met. I have come to realise that, to care for that person, it may require the development of dependency between me and the person in need of care, if it is to ever address the underlying difficulty. In other words, a core part of the 'treatment' may focus not around trying to break up an important relationship that the service user has, but instead to provide one to them that may, over time, become more important. Appropriate care might involve the offer of an opportunity for the individual to experience the sort of dependency that so many of us took for granted to the point where we did not even know we had it, but which has underpinned all of our health and well-being since. The absence of healthy, life-giving, dependent relationships is so often written through the life stories of people I see who come into contact with homeless and substance-misuse services, but as they are presented with overshadowing symptoms such as homelessness and substance misuse, and as we organise and name our services around these symptoms, we run the risk of not only missing the underlying need, but, through processes such as discharge and other terminations of the care relationship, of maintaining the sort of negative relational experiences that gave rise to the presenting difficulties in the first place.

You clearly see problems with the ways that services are organised; are there other ways that we can get it wrong?
Other examples can be found in the language that service providers use to describe the relationship they have with those they are working with. For example, those working in health, housing and social care often use the words 'non-engagement' to describe the relationships where they feel

the service user is not relating to the service in the way that the service would like them to. It is when services then act on these feelings by doing such things as discharging or excluding a patient that relational damage can be replicated. The service user who engages with a service by doing things such as not turning up to appointments, or by turning up late or in an intoxicated manner, always runs the risk of having their care terminated through being excluded, discharged or otherwise disengaged. It is rare to find a service that spends time reflecting on the experience of being stood up by a service user, and rarer still to find a service that might use those reflections to inform their understanding of the life difficulties of the individual in an attempt to stay in a care-giving relationship with them.

Perhaps the not-turning-upness is telling us something about the individual's experience of neglect? Perhaps we are being invited to feel what it is like to be abandoned, left and not cared for? What if the missed appointments are telling us something about the person's experience of disappointment and unreliability, or just giving us a concrete communication about the terror the individual feels when they think someone might be interested in them? Services can become very confused by individuals who both demand care and then routinely do not make use of the care that is provided. Whether that care comes in the form of a house, a keyworker appointment or a medical procedure, service providers can get very frustrated when, after going to great lengths to provide the requested care, it is then rebuked, abused or abandoned. When people who have experienced high levels of distress communicate their history by behaving in deeply ambivalent ways, it is understandable that services might use phrases such as 'non-engagement' as a way of getting rid of the ambivalent behaviour, and the feelings of frustration, impotence and confusion that ambivalence can evoke, but in doing so they may well exacerbate the very life problem they are trying to treat as they re-enact an excluding and rejecting dynamic.

Ambivalence about intimacy, closeness and trust within human relationships is both a very understandable consequence of early adversity and trauma, and a real barrier to receiving care. Most services are designed by the relatively healthy – the unambivalent. Services are typically designed to assume a healthy internal world where an individual can make use of a care relationship in a straightforward and uncomplicated way. It asks that they turn up on time, sit in waiting rooms and then go into other rooms with shut doors to speak to somebody who is interested in their various vulnerabilities. As relatively healthy carers, we can find ourselves drawn to people who make use of the care as we have designed it, and can start to feel frustrated, defeated and even abused by those who do not relate to care in a straightforward manner. It is at these points that we can find ourselves responding to these feelings by doing such things as discharging the service user, deeming them unsuitable or unready for the service, or calling them names such as 'personality disorder'. (You can bet any money you like that the term 'personality disorder' was not made up by a service user.) All such responses can serve to replicate and exacerbate the relational experiences and difficulties of the service user.

You refer to emotions frequently, can you expand on this?
The feelings and emotional responses of services and those working within them should not be underestimated. They play a significant factor in how care is organised, who it is given to and even if it is given at all. As mentioned, for those who express their lives in distressing ways, they may be subject to less care than those whose anguish is expressed in ways that evoke other sorts of feelings. For example, someone who has seen it as important to self-harm may find themselves in a hospital-type situation being offered a range of care and treatment options, whereas someone who has harmed someone else may find themselves involved with the criminal justice system where they may not receive quite the care received by the self-harmer. Both individuals may be in a great deal of distress. Indeed, both may even have experienced very similar backgrounds of trauma, neglect and abuse, but the care and treatment they receive is not informed by this, but instead organised around and overshadowed by how that distress is communicated. For many, this means that their history and life experience – what happened to them – are lost because the ways in which their distress is expressed does not evoke feelings such as sympathy, curiosity and compassion. Our responses are often markedly different to different people, often because of how their current way of relating makes us feel. This can occur even when the underlying relational and developmental experiences, which individuals have had no choice over, are very similar.

Health and social care provision typically operates from a relational model that is rarely articulated, but at its heart has an assumption that all service users can relate to, and make use of, care in a straightforward and anxiety-free way. It assumes that people in need of care have little or no anxiety about being needy or vulnerable, and have an internal model of care that is free from abuse, neglect and pain. Policies and procedures that determine inclusion and exclusion from the care relationship are then derived from this basic assumption. This somewhat institutionally-autistic idea can prove very problematic for those whose responses to care and interest are, by virtue of the trauma and adversity they have experienced in their developmental experiences of care, very, very far from straightforward. Trauma, disturbance and adversity in the earliest experiences of others can lead to later care relationships that appear complicated, ambivalent and even destructive.

From what I have witnessed, health and social care services do not often deal well with extreme ambivalence. A failure of the service to understand, bear or tolerate the way in which the service user is actually relating to care can easily lead to excluding and limiting responses. The relationship chokes, and the service user has another experience of being excluded, which typically serves to increase their anxiety about future contacts with care. This is a drama that can be seen playing out in many healthcare settings as individuals are excluded, discharged and disengaged because of the distressing ways in which they relate to the service: the aggressive patient is excluded from the service; the non-attending engager is discharged for missing appointments; and the chronically intoxicated is told she is not suitable for treatment. In each case, the relational experience that is played out re-enacts and reinforces the internally held relational experiences that cause so much distress to the individual. The service response may not go as far as worsening the individual's psychological state, but can certainly play a part in maintaining it.

For those individuals who have experienced high levels of anxiety, pain and suffering in their early experiences of care, then the relationship that the individual has *with care itself* can become the life-limiting problem. The difficulties that the person has in the formation and maintenance of life-giving relationships in their general life can be intensified when they are in contact with a service specifically organised around care. It seems like a horrible dilemma can occur for the individual whereby their need for care increases as they struggle to get those care needs met, but their phobia of the care relationship and the subsequent choking dynamic mean they cannot get the care they need. The trauma and adversity they have experienced has left them understandably extremely ambivalent about relationships, and in particular about relationships that are built around an offer of care and/or dependency. This core relational impairment can lead to a severe and at times life-limiting double disability. Firstly, the individual's needs may be extremely high due to the fact that they have been unmet for so long. The person may literally be starving for attention and care, which can come across in high levels of demands and expectations towards a service. Secondly, however, the person cannot make use of the care as it is provided because of the anxieties and fears its presence evokes. This can become manifest in the individual not turning up to demanded-for treatment, attacking and dismissing offers of care, and in general seeming to undermine or defeat the efforts of the service. Deep anxiety and ambivalence about care are often only seen through these behaviours.

The one thing I've observed that the individual finds very difficult to do, because of their phobia around care, is tell the carer how scared they are of them. The fears can become manifest in a range of other behaviours such as aggression, neglect and abuse. I have found that it is really not obvious that the person may be anxious; their behaviour often does not look like anxiety. In this regard, it is something of an invisible impairment. Unfortunately, when impairment is invisible in this way it is at much greater risk of becoming a life-limiting disability than a more visible one. We would, for example, never think about providing stair-only access to a clinic for those who are dependent on wheelchairs, but we seem to organise care in a way that is inaccessible to people who have experienced high levels of trauma. There are very few services organised and designed for people who struggle to make use of services, and even fewer for those who are felt to be actively destructive and antagonistic towards care. We have many services organised around presenting symptoms, but much fewer that are organised around an understanding of a difficulty in the relationship with care itself. We have eating-disorder services, substance-misuse services and alcohol-problem clinics; we do not, however, have relational development services.

Nothing excludes like a label. The names and labels we attach to particular presentations and their respective clinics can serve to exclude those who bring anxiety into care. The arbitrary categories and classifications we give to those presenting psychological distress, and to the places we ask to meet them in, focus our minds on the presenting symptoms to the exclusion of the relational processes that underpin and describe all care transactions. For those whose expressions of distress do not happily fall into a preordained category, and as such are understood as being 'just bad', 'manipulative' or 'at it', there is a price to be paid in the form of further health inequality as the services move care away from them towards those who are expressing their distress 'properly'.

You have talked a lot about services that do not meet the needs of people who have experienced adverse childhood experiences and trauma; what is the solution?

A psychologically informed approach places an interest and analysis of the relational elements of care at the heart of its operation. It acknowledges the psychological and emotional needs of the individuals it finds itself in relationships with, and attempts to organise itself around a sound and grounded understanding of those needs. It recognises the relationship between itself and those with whom it works as the central vehicle for care and change, acknowledging that the psychosocial background of the individual may have impacted upon the ways in which they relate to themselves and others. The shift here is one away from a complete interest in the content of *what* we do, to a shared interest between that and the relational and structural processes involved in *how* we do it. It seeks to provide a physical environment that feels safe and secure, and aims to be informed by a coherent and evidence-based psychological framework. Recognising that the relational dynamics of the work may not always be straightforward, a reflective practice process for service providers is a central component of the approach. For those of us who can form and maintain life-giving relationships as easily as we can breathe, it can be very easy to forget, or not recognise in the first place, that relationships underpin all of the work we do in health and social care. Because we do not necessarily fully acknowledge or notice our own relation history as being of importance to us, it becomes easy to neglect the degree of relational deficit others may have experienced. Like our healthy breathing, we can become unaware about the importance of our relationships to our own health and well-being when they are going well and running in an automatic and invisible fashion, and in doing so can become ignorant to the fact that not all of those we provide care and support to are afforded this seemingly effortless ability.

This kind of work also seems to be very emotionally demanding on health and social care practitioners; what can be done to support them?

All health and social care is relational, and the reflective practice process provides a regular and protected forum in which staff can speak honestly about their relational experiences, and through reflection try and use their experiences to inform future care in a way that aims to maximise the well-being of both staff and service user. The reflective practice process can be particularly useful and important when working with individuals who have experienced high levels of adversity and trauma, and who express some of this history in ways that do not initially evoke thought, curiosity or sympathy. When staff feel threatened, when they feel abused and hurt, and when they feel used and mistreated, their first emotional responses are rarely, and understandably, not empathy, care and concern. The reflective practice process is designed to help staff make some sense of why some people might find it important to relate in ways that are frightening, alarming and destructive, and bring thought and understanding to situations that can often evoke reactive and unprocessed responses. This can be hard work. Staying thoughtful about relationships that have evoked fear and harm can be difficult and counter to our ordinary human responses, but it is crucial if services are to remain in a position that carries a potential for health and development. At its most simple then, I understand a psychologically informed service to take as full an account as possible of the psychological and emotional development of those who seek care from it, and to work hard to ensure that it does not re-enact the adverse relational dynamics that may have left the service user in need of a service in the first place. The reflective practice process is at the heart of this, attempting to shine a light on the invisible relational processes underpinning all of our work.

The literature on ACEs is clear about the protective nature of having at least one secure and trustworthy relationship in childhood. This data highlights the importance of secure relationships in the development of good mental and physical well-being, and provides evidence as to why and how a psychologically informed approach views relationships as the key component of enabling change. The approach can serve to validate and legitimise the development and maintenance of relationships as being an important, if not fundamental, part of our work. The care relationship is often de-emphasised in mainstream care provision in contrast to the elevated place specific treatments and interventions are afforded. It is very common in homeless and mental health services, for example, to hear about treatment of depression, and the addressing of homelessness, but much rarer to hear talk of the development of relationships and the building of healthy dependency and trust.

It seems to be easily forgotten that there is, at any one time, an ongoing, massive, international, multi-site trial demonstrating the health and life-giving properties of relationships. It is called 'the family'. It comes in many shapes, sizes and configurations, but for the most part seems to produce, in the absence of any specific or special training for those providing the care, good outcomes for the majority of individuals brought up within it. Family studies show clearly how the nature and quality of the relational dynamics within the group describe the health and well-being of its members, but interestingly, when it comes to providing professional care later on in life, the importance of relationships seems to become a minority interest. This can often leave a range of 'non-specialist' care staff with an idea that all of the good stuff is being done elsewhere and by other people: for example, by highly trained professionals in specialist clinics to which individuals are referred as part of their treatment. When working in this area, a common experience is to hear staff diminish their work by starting a description of their activities with 'But I just ...' or 'But all I really do is ...', and then go on to describe the provision of a thoughtful, stable, reliable, trustworthy, coherent, boundaried and dependable relationship over time, as if it were something utterly trivial. The psychologically informed approach challenges this perception and, with proper reflective practice processes in place, demonstrates that a good psychological understanding can be owned and shared by everyone, and that good psychological care can be provided by staff and service providers at all levels. It is widely accepted within the area of choking management that a very broad spectrum of people can be trained in the business of cardiopulmonary resuscitation (CPR) and can, with a little regular support and training, be in a position to save a life if need be. The psychologically informed approach takes a similar view on choking in relationships. There is a very broad spectrum of people, across a wide range of sectors, professions and services – from teachers, to prison staff, to doctors to mothers – who, with a little training and support, can provide life-giving relationships to individuals who previous to that point may have had little or no experience of such a thing.

Conclusion

In this chapter, relationships are regarded as the psychological equivalent of breathing. We all have multiple and complex psychological needs, but thankfully for most of us we can get those needs met through the basic processes of relating, something we do as naturally and effortlessly as breathing in a friendly, oxygen-rich atmosphere. However, there are those for whom the basic processes are not straightforward, and it is only through the analysis of relationships that repeatedly choke, and the continued provision of relationships that carry the potential for health, that the levels of exclusion and health inequality experienced by some of the most vulnerable members of our communities will ever be addressed.

CHAPTER 8

Conclusion

This chapter will summarise the book and bring together the discussions and debates by suggesting areas for further exploration as well as giving recommendations for health and social care policy and practice and areas for further research.

The first paragraph of this book began with the image of 'strangers on the streets', where the undocumented migrant and the local citizen bed down for the night in the doorways of luxury stores. The experiences of homelessness for the migrant and the local are not positioned as two distinct fields, but together as the result of global, national, local and individual circumstances. While the health needs of the local citizen and the migrant are different, when they become homeless – particularly sleeping rough – health experiences merge. In response, international, national and local responses should consider migrant and citizen health needs together, where assessment and interventions are implemented by framing people experiencing homelessness as an 'ordinary' manifestation of global health inequalities, neoliberalism and stigma, rather than as an 'extraordinary' category of people. To live without a home – somewhere safe, secure, private and beyond public scrutiny – is a breach of human rights, regardless of how someone came to that place.

Governments continue to focus on either statutory homeless figures or to react to the visible sight of rough sleepers, and yet there are multiple ways that homelessness is hidden: through policies that do not recognise undocumented migrants; through strategies people use to negotiate relationships that protect from greater dangers on the streets; and by entering the informal economy that brings dangers of exploitation and abuse. Approaches to improve the health and well-being of people experiencing homelessness should frame homelessness for migrants in the same ways as that of citizens, not as a separate research, policy or practice discourse.

Policymakers, practitioners, health and care organisations and third-sector initiatives need to work together to ensure access to housing and healthcare services and to destigmatise trauma-informed care.

People with lived experience should be at the centre of planning, policy and healthcare initiatives so that lessons can be learnt and the nuanced experiences of homelessness more clearly understood. While drug developments in the fields of hepatitis C and HIV have been undoubtedly transformative, solutions to improve the health and well-being of people experiencing homelessness are also needed that focus on the impact of stigmatisation, racism and social exclusion. These should be developed with and by people with lived experience, both migrants and citizens, to reframe homelessness as an experience rather than a 'label'.

People who experience homelessness are often framed in healthcare discourse as vulnerable and in need of help – often by hostile media – and so new frames need to be developed, where stories of resilience and resistance are foregrounded. Health and social care initiatives should harness this resilience and develop services based on respect and dignity, rather than vulnerability and 'chaotic lives'. As understandings of the impact of trauma, ACEs and violence deepen, new and 'psychologically informed' environments and ways of working should be developed to ensure that services provide safety, security, respect and dignity.

Finally, as understandings of the pathways into and out of homelessness develop, a more intersectional approach to health should be developed, to understand the particular nuanced ways that women, young people, forced migrants and people who identify as LGBT experience and negotiate homelessness; and, in doing so, more appropriate services and support could be delivered. While we had space to consider only these particular identities, further work is ongoing to explore the experiences of homelessness for people with disability, war veterans, sex workers, gypsies and travellers and a range of other marginalised groups. An intersectional approach to health and well-being is vital to ensure 'hidden' experiences of homelessness are identified and services developed appropriately.

Homelessness is a global challenge and the result of global pressures that are manifest on local streets, but the solutions are embedded in the global economy, national policy, local practice and individual life experiences. Certainly, policymakers are correct to look for an 'end to homelessness', but, in order to achieve this admirable goal, homelessness will be eradicated only when global inequalities are tackled and the social gradient in health is flattened. Complex causes of ill health require us to work at multiple levels and in divergent ways in order to find multiple solutions to health inequalities, and only then will people meet in homes and places of safety, privacy and belonging, rather than as 'strangers on the streets'.

REFERENCES

Abdulkadir, J., Azzudin, A., Buick, A., Curtice, L., Dzingisau, M., Easton, D., Frew, C., Glinski, J., Hollliday, D., Knifton, L., McLaughlin, D., Auinn, N. and Ramsay, D. (2016) *What Do You Mean, I Have the Right to Health? Participatory Action Research on Health and Human Rights*, Glasgow: Strathclyde University. Available from URL: https://strathprints.strath.ac.uk/58209/1/ Abdulkadir_etal_IPPI_2016_What_do_you_mean_I_have_a_right_to_ health.pdf (accessed 8 May 2018)

Abubakar, I., Devakumar, D., Madise, N., Sammonds, P., Groce, N., Zimmerman, C., Aldridge, R. W., Clark, J. and Horton, R. (2016) 'UCL–Lancet Commission on Migration and Health', *The Lancet*, Vol. 388, No. 10050, pp. 1141–2; doi: 10.1016/S0140–6736(16)31581–1

Agamben, G. (1998) *Homo Sacer: Sovereign Power and Bare Life*, Stanford, CA: Stanford University Press

Agier, M. (2010) 'Forced migration and asylum: stateless citizens today', in Andebent, C. and Dorian, M. K. (eds) *Migration in a Globalised World*, Amsterdam: Amsterdam University Press, p. 183

Ahmad, F., Driver, N., McNally, M. J. and Stewart, D. E. (2009) '"Why doesn't she seek help for partner abuse?" An exploratory study with South Asian immigrant women', *Social Science & Medicine*, Vol. 69, No. 4, pp. 613–22; doi: 10.1016/j.socscimed.2009.06.011

Ahmet, A. (2013) 'Home sites: The location(s) of "home" for young men', *Urban Studies*, Vol. 50, No. 3, p. 621e634; doi: 10.1177/0042098012468896

Ahrens, S. (2016) 'Understanding sport as the expansion of capabilities: The homeless world cup and street soccer (Scotland)' (Unpublished PhD), Edinburgh: University of Edinburgh. Available at URL: www.era.lib.ed.ac.uk/ bitstream/handle/1842/21008/Ahrens2016.pdf?sequence=3&isAllowed=y (accessed 14 March 2019)

Alaazi, D. A., Masuda, J. R., Evans, J. and Disasio, J. (2015) 'Therapeutic landscapes of home: Exploring indigenous people's experiences of a Housing First intervention in Winnipeg', *Social Science & Medicine*, Vol. 147, pp. 30–7; doi: 10.1016/j.socscimed.2015.10.057

Albert Kennedy Trust (2015)) 'LGBT youth homelessness: A UK national scoping of cause, prevalence, response & outcome' (online). Available from URL: www.akt.org.uk/Handlers/Download.ashx?IDMF=c0f29272–512a-45e8– 9f9b-0b76e477baf1 (accessed 6 June 2016)

Aldridge, R. W., Story, A., Hwang, S. W., Nordentoft, M., Luchenski, S. A., Hartwell, G., Tweed, E. J., Lewer, D., Katikireddi, S. V. and Hayward, A. C. (2017) 'The health impact of social exclusion: A systematic review and meta-analysis of morbidity and mortality data from homeless, prison, sex work and substance use disorder populations in high-income countries', *The Lancet*; doi:

10.1016/S0140-6736(17)31869-X

Ali, S. H. (2010) 'Tuberculosis, homelessness, and the politics of mobility', Canadian Journal of Urban Research, Vol. 19, No. 2, pp. 80–107

Allan, B. and Sakamoto, I. (2014) 'Helpers, not helpless: Honouring strength, wisdom and vision of Aboriginal women experiencing homelessness or marginal housing', in Guirguis-Younger, M., McNeil, R. and Hwang, S. W. (eds) Homelessness and Health in Canada, Ottawa: University of Ottawa Press, pp. 36–57

Allsopp, J., Sigona, N. and Phillimore, J. (2014) Poverty Among Refugees and Asylum Seekers in the UK: An Evidence and Policy Review, Birmingham: University of Birmingham, Institute for Research into Superdiversity

Alpak, G., Unal, A., Bulbul, F., Sagaltici, E., Bez, Y., Altindag, A., Dalkilic, A. and Savas, H. (2015) 'Post-traumatic stress disorder among Syrian refugees in Turkey: A cross-sectional study', International Journal of Psychiatry in Clinical Practice, Vol. 19, No. 1, pp. 45–50; doi: 10.3109/13651501.2014.961930

Amazon Studios (2017) 'Human flow' (online). Available from URL: www. amazon.com/Human-Flow-Ai-Weiwei/dp/B075VJNKZC (accessed 12 June 2018)

Amin, A. (2012) Land of strangers, Cambridge: Polity Press

Amin, A. (2013) 'Land of strangers', Identities, Vol. 20, No. 1, pp. 1–8; doi: 10.1080/1070289x,2012.732544

Anagnostopoulos, D., Giannakopoulos, G. and Christodoulou, N. (2016) 'A compounding mental health crisis: Reflections from the Greek experience with Syrian refugees', American Journal of Psychiatry, Vol. 173, No. 11, pp. 1081–2; doi: 10.1176/appi.ajp. 2016.16060667

Anderson, B., Gibney, M. and Paoletti, E. (2013) 'Citizenship, deportation and the boundaries of belonging', Citizenship Studies, Vol. 15, No. 5, pp. 547–63; doi: 10.1080/13621025.2011.583787

Anderson, I., Baptista, I., Wolf, J. R. L. M., Edgar, B., Sapounakis, A. and Schoibl, H. (2006) The Changing Role of Service Provision: Barriers of Access to Health Services for Homeless People, Brussels: FEANTSA

Arendt, H. (1973) The Origins of Totalitarianism, Vol. 348 Houghton Mifflin Harcourt

Arendt, M., Munk-Jørgensen, P., Sher, L. and Jensen, S. O. (2011) 'Mortality among individuals with cannabis, cocaine, amphetamine, MDMA, and opioid use disorders: A nationwide follow-up study of Danish substance users in treatment', Drug Alcohol Dependency, Vol. 114, pp. 134–9: doi: 10.3109/10826084.2013.786731

Arnold, K. R. (2004) Homelessness, Citizenship, and Identity: The Uncanniness of Late Modernity, Albany, NY: State University of New York Press

ASAP (2008) Not Destitute Enough: A Report Documenting UKBA's Failure to Apply the Correct Definitions of Destitution in Asylum Support Decisions, London: Asylum Support Appeals Project. Available from URL: http://stillhuman-stillhere.files.wordpress.com/2009/01/asap_not_destitute_enough_dec_2008.pdf (accessed 14 January 2014)

Asten, L., Verhaest, I., Lamzira, S., Hernandez-Aguado, I., Zangerle, R., Faroudy Boufassa, F., Rezza, G., Broers, B., Robertson, R., Brettle, R. O., McMenamin, J., Prins, M., Cochrane, A., Simmonds, P. and Coutinho, R. A. (2004) 'European and Italian seroconverter studies: Spread of hepatitis C virus among European injection drug users infected with HIV: A phylogenetic analysis', *The Journal of Infectious Diseases*, Vol. 189, No. 2, pp. 292–302; doi: 10.1086/380821

Aubry, T., Goering, P., Veldhuizen, S., Adair, C. E., Bourque, J., Distasio, J., Latimer, E., Stergiopoulos, V., Somers, J., Streiner, D. L. and Tsemberis, S. (2015) 'A multiple-city RCT of housing first with assertive community treatment for homeless Canadians with serious mental illness', *Psychiatric Services*, Vol. 67, No. 3, pp. 275–81

Australian Bureau of Statistics (2018) 'Homelessness statistics' (online). Available from URL: http://abs.gov.au (accessed 24 September 2018)

Bacchi, C. (2009) *Analysing Policy: What's the Problem Represented to Be?*, Sydney: Pearson

Baggett, T. P., Hwang, S. W., O'Connell, J. J., Porneala, B. C., Stringfellow, E. J., Singer, D. E. and Rigotti, N. A. (2013) 'Mortality among homeless adults in Boston: Shifts in causes of death over a 15-year period', *JAMA Internal Medicine*, Vol. 173, pp. 189–95

Bambra, C. (2011) 'Recession, unemployment and health', in *Work, Worklessness, and the Political Economy of Health*, Oxford: Oxford University Press

Bambra, C. (2012) 'Reducing health inequalities: New data suggest that the English strategy was partially successful', *Journal of Epidemiology and Community Health*, Vol. 66, No. 7, p. 662; doi: 10.1136/jech-2011-200945

Baptista, I. (2010) 'Women and homelessness in Europe', in O'Sullivan, E., Busch-Geertsema, V., Quilgars, D. and Pleace, N. (eds), *Homelessness Research in Europe*, Brussels: FEANTSA, pp. 163–86

Baran, S. J. and Davis, D. K. (2008) *Mass Communication Theory: Foundations, Ferment, and Future*, 5th edn, Boston, MA: Wadsworth Cengage Learning

Bauer, G. R. (2014) 'Incorporating intersectionality theory into population health research methodology: Challenges and the potential to advance health equity', *Social Science & Medicine*, Vol. 110, pp. 10–17; doi: 10.1016/j.socscimed.2014.03.022

Bauman, Z. (2007) *Liquid Times: Living in an Age of Uncertainty*, Cambridge: Polity Press

Bauman, Z. (2013) *Liquid Modernity*, Oxford: Wiley

Bauman, Z. (2017) *Strangers at Our Door*, Cambridge: Polity Press

Baynes, C. (2018) 'Council branded as "inhumane" after installing metal bars on benches to stop homeless people sleeping on them' (online). Available from URL: www.independent.co.uk/news/uk/home-news/bournemouth-council-installs-metal-bars-benches-homeless-rough-sleepers-inhumane-crisis-stuart-a8186121.html (accessed 5 February 2019)

BBC (British Broadcasting Corporation) (2016) 'Calais death: Relatives of killed boy, 14, tell of his last moments' (online). Available from URL: www.bbc.co.uk/news/uk-37423039 (accessed 10 January 2018)

Bean, T. M., Eurelings-Bontekoe, E. and Spinhoven, P. (2007) 'Course and predictors of mental health of unaccompanied refugee minors in the Netherlands: One year follow-up', *Social Science & Medicine*, Vol. 64, No. 6, pp. 1204–15;

doi: 10.1016/j.socscimed.2006.11.010

Beck, U. (2015) *The Reinvention of Politics: Rethinking Modernity in the Global Social Order*, Cambridge: Polity Press.

Becker, H. (1966) *Social Problems: A Modern Approach*, New York: Wiley

Beijer, U., Wolf, A. and Fazel, S. (2012) 'Prevalence of tuberculosis, hepatitis C virus, and HIV in homeless people: A systematic review and meta-analysis', *The Lancet Infectious Diseases*, Vol. 12, No. 11, pp. 859–70; doi: 10.1016/S1473-3099(12)70177-9

Bellis, M. A., Lowey, H., Leckenby, N., Hughes, K. and Harrison, D. (2013) 'Adverse childhood experiences: Retrospective study to determine their impact on adult health behaviours and health outcomes in a UK population', *Journal of Public Health*, Vol. 36, No. 1, pp. 81–91; doi: 10.1093/pubmed/fdt038

Best, R. (2010) 'Situation or social problem: The influence of events on media coverage of homelessness', *Social Problems*, Vol. 57, No. 1, pp. 74–91; doi: 10.1525/sp.2010.57.1.74

Betts, A. and Collier, P. (2017) *Refuge: Transforming a Broken Refugee System*, London: Allen Lane

Bhandari, R., Warren, J., Kasim, A. and Bambra, C. (2017) 'Geographical inequalities in health in a time of austerity: Baseline findings from Stockton-on-Tees cohort study', *Health & Place*, Vol. 48, pp. 111–82; doi: 10.1016/j.healthplace.2017.10.002

Bith-Melander, P., Chowdhury, N., Jindal, C. and Efird, J. T. (2017) 'Trauma affecting Asian-Pacific islanders in the San Francisco bay area', *International Journal of Environmental Research in Public Health*, Vol. 14, p. 1053; doi: 10.3390/ijerph14091053

Blackburn, R. M., Hayward, A., Cornes, M., McKee, M., Lewer, D., Whiteford, M., Menezes, D., Luchenski, S., Story, A., Denaxas, S. and Tinelli, M. (2017) 'Outcomes of specialist discharge coordination and intermediate care schemes for patients who are homeless: Analysis protocol for a population-based historical cohort', *BMJ Open*, Vol. 7, No. 12, p. e019282; doi: 10.1136/bmjopen-2017-019282

Blitz, B. K., d'Angelo, A., Kofman, E. and Montagna, N. (2017) 'Health challenges in refugee reception: Dateline Europe 2016', *International Journal of Environmental Research in Public Health*, Vol. 14, p. 1484; doi: 10.3390/ijerph14121484

Bloch, A. (2013) 'Living in fear: Rejected asylum seekers living as irregular migrants in England', *Journal of Ethnic and Migration Studies*, Vol. 40, No. 10, pp. 1507–25; doi: 10.1080/1369183X.2013.859070

Bollini, P., Pampallona, S.,Wanner, P. and Kupelnick, B. (2009) 'Pregnancy outcome of migrant women and integration policy: A systematic review of the international literature', *Social Science & Medicine*, Vol. 68, No. 3, pp. 452–61; doi: 10.1016/j.socscimed.2008.10.018

Bosworth, M. (2016) 'The impact of immigration detention on mental health: A literature review', Criminal Justice, Borders and Citizenship Research Paper No. 2732892 (online). Available from URL: https://papers.ssrn.com/sol3/papers.cfm?abstract_id=2732892 (accessed 12 August 2017)

Bourdieu, P. (1991) *Language and Symbolic Power*, Cambridge: Polity Press

Bourdieu, P. (2011) *On Television*, Cambridge: Polity Press

Bowleg, L. (2012) The problem with the phrase women and minorities: Inter-sectionality – an important theoretical framework for public health', *American Journal of Public Health*, Vol. 102, No. 7, pp. 1267–73; doi: 10.2105/AJPH.2012.300750

Bowpitt, G., Dwyer, P., Sundin, E. and Weinstein, M. (2011) 'Comparing men's and women's experiences of multiple exclusion homelessness', *Social Policy and Society*, Vol. 10, No. 4, pp. 537–46; doi: 10.1017/S1474746411000285

Bradby, H., Humphris, R., Newall, D. and Phillimore, J. (2015) 'Public health aspects of migrant health: A review of the evidence on health status for refugees and asylum seekers in the European Region', Health Evidence Network synthesis report 44, Copenhagen: WHO Regional Office for Europe. Available from URL: www.euro.who.int/__data/assets/pdf_file/0004/289246/WHO-HEN-Report-A5-2-Refugees_FINAL.pdf (accessed 24 June 2017)

Bradby, H., Green, G., Davison, C. and Krause, K. (2017) 'Is superdiversity a useful concept in European medical sociology?', *Frontiers Sociology*, Vol. 1, p. 17; doi: 10.3389/fsoc.2016.00017

Bradley-Engen, M. S. (2011) 'Stigma and the deviant identity', in Bryant, C. D. (ed.) (2011) *The Routledge Handbook of Deviant Behaviour*, London: Routledge, pp. 190–4

Bramley, G. and Fitzpatrick, S. (2018) WHomelessness in the UK: who is most at risk?', *Housing Studies*, Vol. 33, No. 1, pp. 96–116; doi: 10.1080/02673037.2017.1344957

Bramley, G., Fitzpatrick, S., Edwards, J., Ford, D., Johnsen, S., Sosenko, F. and Watkins, D. (2015) 'Hard edges: Mapping severe and multiple disadvantage in England' (online). Available from URL: https://lankellychase.org.uk/resources/publications/hard-edges (accessed 11 February 2019)

Braubach, M. and Fairburn, J. (2010) 'Social inequities in environmental risks associated with housing and residential location: A review of evidence', *European Journal of Public Health*, Vol. 20, No. 1, pp. 36–42; doi: 10.1093/eurpub/ckp221

Breedvelt, J. F. (2016) *Psychologically Informed Environments: A Literature Review*, London: Mental Health Foundation/St Mungo's

Briggs, D., Rhodes, T., Marks, D., Kimber, J., Holloway, G. and Jones, S. (2009) 'Injecting drug use and unstable housing: Scope for structural interventions in harm reduction', *Drugs: Education Prevention and Policy*, Vol. 16, No. 5, pp. 436–50

British Red Cross and Boaz Trust (2013) *A Decade of Destitution: Time to Make Change*, Manchester: British Red Cross

Brown, P., Morris, G., Scullion, L. and Somerville, P. (2008) 'Losing and finding a home: homelessness, multiple exclusion and everyday lives', Economic and Social Research Council Research report (online). Available from URL: http://usir.salford.ac.uk/35876/1/Losing%20and%20Finding%20a%20Home.pdf (accessed 8 May 2017)

Brown, R. T., Kimes, R. V., Guzman, D. and Kushel, M. (2010) 'Health care access and utilization in older versus younger homeless adults', *Journal of Health Care for the Poor and Underserved*, Vol. 21, pp. 1060–70

Brown, R. T., Kiely, D. K., Bharel, M. and Mitchell, S. L. (2012) 'Geriatric syndromes in older homeless adults', *Journal of General Internal Medicine*, Vol. 27, pp. 16–22; doi: 10.1007/s11606-011-1848-9

Brown, R. T., Kiely, D. K., Bharel, M., Mitchell, S. L. (2013) 'Factors associated with geriatric syndromes in older homeless adults', *Journal of Health Care Poor Underserved*, Vol. 24, pp. 456–68

Buck, P. O., Toro, P. A. and Ramos, M. A. (2004) 'Media and professional interest in homelessness over 30 years (1974–2003)', *Analyses of Social Issues and Public Policy*, Vol. 4, No. 1, pp. 151–71; doi: 10.1111/j.1530-2415.2004.00039.x

Bull, M., Schindeler, E., Berkman, D. and Ransley, J. (2012) 'Sickness in the System of Long-term Immigration Detention', *Journal of Refugee Studies*, Vol. 26, No. 1, pp. 47–68; doi: 10.1093/jrs/fes017

Burke-Harris, N. B. (2018) *The Deepest Well: Healing the Long-Term Effects of Childhood Adversity*, New York, NY: Houghton Mifflin Harcourt

Burnett, A. and Peel, M. (2001) 'What brings asylum seekers to the United Kingdom?', *British Medical Journal*, Vol. 322, No. 7284, pp. 485–8

Busch-Geertsema, V. (2013) *Housing First Europe: Final Report*, Bremen/Brussels: European Union Programme for Employment and Social Solidarity. Available from URL: www.habitat.hu/files/FinalReportHousingFirstEurope.pdf (accessed 11 February 2019)

Busch-Geertsema, V., Benjaminsen, L., Filipovic Harst, M. and Pleasce, N. (2014) *Extent and Profile of Homelessness in European Member States: A Statistical Update*, Brussels: FEANTSA

Busch-Geertsema, V., Culhane, D. and Fitzpatrick, S. (2016) 'Developing a global framework for conceptualising and measuring homelessness', *Habitat International*, Vol. 55, pp. 124–32; doi: 10.1016/j.habitatint.2016.03.004

Business Standard (2017) 'India's Inc bets on 7% GDP growth in 2017–18' (online). Available from URL: www.business-standard.com/article/economy-policy/india-inc-bets-on-7-gdp-growth-in-2017–18-117120201044_1.html (accessed 12 June 2018)

Calder, M. J., Hansard, A., Richter, S., Burns, K. K. and Mao, Y. (2011) 'Framing homelessness for the Canadian public: The news media and homelessness', *Canadian Journal of Urban Research*, Vol. 20, No. 2, pp. 1–19

Canavan, R., Barry, M. M., Matanov, A., Barros, H., Gabor, E., Greacen, T., Holcnerová, P., Kluge, U., Nicaise, P., Moskalewicz, J., Díaz-Olalla, J. M., Straßmayr, C., Schene, A. H., Soares, J. J.F, Gaddini, A. and Priebe, S. (2012) 'Service provision and barriers to care for homeless people with mental health problems across 14 European capital cities', *BMC Health Services Research*, Vol. 12, No. 1, p. 222

Carter, M. (2007) *Towards an ESRC Research Programme on Multiple Exclusion Homelessness*, London: Homeless Link/Department for Communities

Case, D. (1996) 'Contributions of journeys away to the definition of home: An empirical study of a dialectical process', *Journal of Environmental Psychology*, Vol. 16, No. 1, pp. 1–15

Casey, R., Goudie, R. and Reeve, K. (2008) 'Homeless women in public places:

Strategies of resistance', *Housing Studies*, Vol. 23, No. 6, pp. 899–916; doi: 10.1080/02673030802416627

Castles, S. (2003) 'Towards a sociology of forced migration and social transformation', *Sociology*, Vol. 37, No. 1, pp. 13–34; doi: 10.1177/0038038503037001384

Castles, S. (2017) 'Migration policies are problematic – because they are about migration', *Ethnic and Racial Studies*, Vol. 40, No. 9, pp. 1538–43; doi: 10.1080/01419870.2017.1308532

Castles, S., De Haas, H. and Miller, M. J. (2013) *The Age of Migration: International Population Movements in the Modern World*, Basingstoke: Macmillan International Higher Education

Caulford, P. and Vali, Y. (2006) 'Providing health care to medically uninsured immigrants and refugees', *Canadian Medical Association Journal*, Vol. 174, No. 9, pp. 1253–4

Centre for Homelessness Impact (2018) 'Evidence gaps and maps' (online). Available from URL: www.homelessnessimpact.org/gap-maps (accessed 14 March 2019)

Chamberlain, C. and Johnson, G. (2013) 'Pathways into adult homelessness', *Journal of Sociology*, Vol. 49, No. 1, pp. 60–77; doi: 10.1177/1440783311422458

Chambers, C., Chiu, S., Katic, M., Kiss, A., Redelmeier, D. A., Levinson, W. and Hwang, S. W. (2013) 'High utilizers of emergency health services in a population-based cohort of homeless adults', *American Journal of Public Health*, Vol. 103, No. S2, pp.S302–S310

Charteris-Black, J. (2006) 'Britain as a container: Immigration metaphors in the 2005 election campaign', *Discourse & Society*, Vol. 17, No. 5, pp. 563–81; doi: 10.1177/0957926506066345

Ciaranello, A. L., Molitor, F., Leamon, M., Kuenneth, C., Tancredi, D., Diamant, A. L. and Kravitz, R. L. (2006) 'Providing health care services to the formerly homeless: A quasi-experimental evaluation', *Journal of Health Care for the Poor and Underserved*, Vol. 17, No. 2, pp. 441–61

Cleveland, J., Kronick, R., Gros, H. and Rousseau, C. (2018) 'Symbolic violence and disempowerment as factors in the adverse impact of immigration detention on adult asylum seekers' mental health,' *International Journal of Public Health*, Vol. 63, No. 8, pp. 1001–8; doi: 10.1007/s00038-018-1121-7

Cloke, P., May, J. and Johnsen, S. (2010) *Swept Up Lives? Re-envisioning the Homeless City*, Chichester: John Wiley & Jones Ltd

Coalition of Homelessness (2016) 'Beating the odds: Annual report' (online). Available from URL: www.cohsf.org/wp-content/uploads/2014/08/2016-ANNUAL-REPORT-COH-1.pdf (accessed 29 June 2017)

Cohen, J. (2008) ' "Safe in our hands?": A study of suicide and self-harm in asylum seekers', *Journal of Forensic and Legal Medicine*, Vol. 5, No. 4, pp. 235–44; doi: 10.1016/j.jflm.2007.11.001

Cohen, N. (2012) *Aging and Homelessness in New York City*, New York, NY: Ravazzin Center on Aging

Collier, P. (2013) *Exodus: Immigration and Multiculturalism in the 21st Century*, Oxford, Oxford University Press

Collier, P. and Betts, A. (2017) *Refuge: Transforming a Broken Refugee System*,

London: Penguin Books

Commission on Housing and Wellbeing (2015) 'A blueprint for Scotland's future' (online). Available from URL: www.housingandwellbeing.org (accessed 10 October 2018)

Coolen, H. and Meesters, C. (2012) 'Editorial special issue: House, home, and dwelling', *Journal of Housing and the Built Environment*, Vol. 27, pp. 1–10

Copeland, A., Kasim, A. and Bambra, C. (2015) 'Grim up north or northern grit? Recessions and the English spatial health divide (1991–2010)', *Journal of Public Health*, Vol. 37, No. 1, pp. 34–9; doi: 10.1093/pubmed/fdu019

Cornes, M., Whiteford, M., Manthorpe, J., Neale, J., Byng, R., Hewett, N., Clark, M., Kilmister, A., Fuller, J., Aldridge, R. and Tinelli, M. (2018) 'Improving hospital discharge arrangements for people who are homeless: A realist synthesis of the intermediate care literature', *Health & Social Care in the Community*, Vol. 26, No. 3, pp. e345–e359; doi: 10.1111/hsc.12474

Corra Foundation (2018) 'Housing First Scotland Fund' (online). Available from URL: www.corra.scot/grant-programmes/housing-first-scotland-fund (accessed 10 October 2018)

Coupar, S. and Mackie, P. (2016) ' "Polishing the diamonds": Addressing adverse childhood experiences in Scotland' (online). Available from URL: www.scot-phn.net/wp-content/uploads/2016/06/2016_05_26-ACE-Report-Final-AF.pdf (accessed 11 February 2019)

Coyne, S. (2018) 'With one voice: Review of arts and homelessness in Scotland' (online). Available from URL: www.with-one-voice.com/sites/default/files/With%20One%20Voice%20Review%20of%20Arts%20and%20Homeless-ness%20in%20Scotland.pdf (accessed 15 June 2018)

Cramb, A. (2018) 'Scottish drugs related deaths hit record high amidst calls for a radical new strategy', *Daily Telegraph*. Available from URL: www.telegraph.co.uk/news/2018/07/03/scottish-drug-deaths-hit-record-high-amid-calls-radical-new (accessed 3 July 2018)

Crane, M. and Joly, M. (2014) 'Older homeless people: Increasing numbers and changing needs', *Reviews in Clinical Gerontology*, Vol. 24, pp. 255–68; doi: 10.1017/S095925981400015X

Crane, M., Warnes, A. M. and Coward, S. (2011) *Moves to Independent Living: Single Homeless People's Experiences and the Outcomes of Resettlement*, Sheffield: Sheffield Institute for Studies on Ageing, University of Sheffield

Crawley, H., Hemmings, J. and Price, N. (2011) *Coping with Destitution: Survival and Livelihood Strategies of Refused Asylum Seekers Living in the UK*, Swansea: Swansea University and Oxfam

Crisis (2011) *Homelessness: A Silent Killer: A Research Briefing on Mortality Amongst Homeless People*, London: Crisis. Available from URL: www.crisis.org.uk/ending-homelessness/homelessness-knowledge-hub/health-and-wellbeing/homelessness-a-silent-killer-2011 (accessed 11 February 2019)

Crisis (2017) *Not Yet Home: A History of Britain's Attempts to Tackle Homelessness*, London: Crisis

Crisis (2018) 'Everybody in: How to end homelessness in Great Britain' (online). Available from URL: www.crisis.org.uk/ending-homelessness/homelessness-knowledge-hub/international-plans-to-end-homelessness/everybody-in-how-to-end-homelessness-in-great-britain-2018 (accessed 17 September 2018)

Cronley, C. (2010) 'Unraveling the social construction of homelessness', *Journal of Human Behavior in the Social Environment*, Vol. 20, No. 2, pp. 319–33; doi: 10.1080/10911350903269955

Crossley, S. (2016). 'From the desk to the front-room? The changing spaces of street-level encounters with the state under austerity', *People Place and Policy Online*, Vol. 10, No. 3, pp. 193–206; doi: 10.3351/ppp.0010.0003.0002

Culhane, D. P., Metraux, S. and Byrne, T. (2011) 'A prevention-centered approach to homelessness assistance: A paradigm shift?', *Housing Policy Debate*, Vol. 21, No. 2, pp. 295–315; doi: 10.1080/10511482.2010.536246

Cuthill, F. (2016) 'Political representation for social justice in nursing: Lessons learned from participant research with destitute asylum seekers in the UK', *Nursing Inquiry*, Vol. 23, No. 3, pp. 211–22; doi: 10.1111/nin.12132

Cuthill, F. (2017) 'Repositioning of "self": Social representation as a part of resilience for destitute asylum seekers in the United Kingdom', *Social Theory and Health*, Vol. 15, pp. 117–26; doi: 10.1057/s41285–016–0025-y

Cuthill, F., Siddiq Abdalla, O. and Bashir, K. (2013) *Between Destitution and a Hard Place: Finding Strength to Survive Refusal from the Asylum System: A Case Study from the North East of England*, Sunderland: University of Sunderland

Darling, J. (2009) 'Becoming bare life: Asylum, hospitality, and the politics of encampment', *Environment and Planning*, Vol. 27, No. 4, p. 649; doi: 10.1068/d10307

Davis, C. (2001) 'Gender and housing', in Harrison, M. and Davis, C. (eds), *Housing, Social Policy and Difference*, Bristol: Polity Press

Davis, M. (1990) *City of Quartz*, London: Vintage

De Andrade, M. (2016) 'Tackling health inequalities through asset-based approaches, co-production and empowerment: Ticking consultation boxes or meaningful engagement with diverse, disadvantaged communities?', *Journal of Poverty and Social Justice*, Vol. 24, No. 2, pp. 127–41

De Certeau, M. (1984) *The Practice of Everyday Life* (trans. Rendall, S.), Berkeley, CA: University of California Press

De Lima, P. (2017) *International Migration: The Wellbeing of Migrants*, Policy and Practice in Health and Social Care No. 21, Edinburgh: Dunedin Academic Press

Department of Health (2010) *Healthcare for Single Homeless People*, London: Office of the Chief Analyst, Department of Health

Department of Health (2013a) *Sustaining Services, Ensuring Fairness: A Consultation on Migrant Access and Financial Contribution to NHS Provision in England*, London: Department of Health

Department of Health (2013b) *Sustaining Services, Ensuring Fairness: Government Response to the Consultation on Migrant Access and Financial Contribution to NHS Provision in England: Equality Analysis*, London: Department of Health

Department of Health (2014) *Overseas Chargeable Patients, NHS Debt and Immigration Rules: Guidance on Administration and Data Sharing*, London: Department of Health

Department of Health (2015) *Guidance on Implementing the Overseas Visitor*

Hospital Charging Regulations 2015, London: Department of Health

Department of Health (2016) *Overseas Chargeable Patients, NHS Debt and Immigration Rules: Guidance on Administration and Data Sharing*, London: Department of Health. Available from URL: https://assets.publishing.service.gov. uk/government/uploads/system/uploads/attachment_data/file/730171/ Overseas_chargeable_patients__NHS_debt_and_immigration_rules.pdf (accessed 14 February 2019)

Department of Health *et al.* (2007) *Drug Misuse and Dependence: UK Guidelines on Clinical Management.* Department of Health (England), the Scottish Government, Welsh Assembly Government, Northern Ireland Executive

Department of Health and Social Security (1980) *The Black Report*, London: Department of Health and Social Security

Derluyn, I. and Broekaert, E. (2008) 'Unaccompanied refugee children and adolescents: The glaring contrast between a legal and a psychological perspective', *International Journal of Law Psychiatry*, Vol. 31, No. 4, pp. 319–30; doi: 10.1016/j.ijlp. 2008.06.006

Devereux, E. (2015) 'Thinking outside the charity box: Media coverage of homelessness', *European Journal of Homelessness*, Vol. 9, No. 2

DeVerteuil, G. (2006) 'The local state of homelessness shelters: Beyond revanchism?', *Cities*, Vol. 23, No. 2, pp. 109–20; doi: 10.1016/j.cities.2005.08.004

DeVerteuil, G., May, J. and Von Mahs, J. (2009) 'Complexity not collapse: Recasting the geographies of homeless in a "punitive" age', *Progress in Human Geography*, Vol. 33, No. 5, pp. 1–21; doi: 10.1177/0309132508104995

Dillabough, J. and Kennelly, J. (2010) *Lost Youth in the Global City: Class, Culture and the Urban Imaginary*, London: Taylor and Francis

Doran, T. and Whitehead, M. (2004) 'Is there a north-south divide in social class inequalities in health in Great Britain? Cross sectional study using data from the 2001 census', *British Medical Journal*, Vol. 328, pp. 1043–5

Dorling, D. (2014) *Inequality and the 1%*, London: Verso

Drummond, P., Mizan, A., Brocx, K. and Wright, B. (2011) 'Barriers to accessing health care services for West African refugee women living in Western Australia', *Health Care for Women International*, Vol. 32, No. 3, pp. 206–24

Dupont, H. J., Kaplan, C. D., Verbraeck, H. T., Braam, R. V. and van de Wijngaart, G. F. (2005) 'Killing time: Drug and alcohol problems among asylum seekers in the Netherlands', *International Journal of Drug Policy*, Vol. 16, No. 1, pp. 27–36

Dupuis, A. and Thorns, D. (1998) 'Home, home ownership and the search for ontological security', *Sociological Review*, Vol. 46, No. 1, pp. 24–47; doi: 10.1111/1467–954X.00088

Durso, L. and Gates, G. (2012) *Serving Our Youth: Findings from a National Survey of Services Providers Working with Lesbian, Gay, Bisexual and Transgender Youth Who Are Homeless or At Risk of Becoming Homeless*, Los Angeles, CA: The Williams Institute with True Colors Fund and The Palette Fund

Dwyer, P. and Somerville, P. (2011) 'Themed section on exploring multiple exclusion homelessness', *Social Policy and Society*, Vol. 10, No. 4, pp. 495–500; doi: 10.1017/S1474746411000248

Dwyer, P., Lewis, H., Scullion, L. and Waite, L. (2011) *Forced Labour and UK*

Immigration Policy: Status Matters?, Salford: University of Salford, Joseph Rowntree Foundation

Edwards, A. (2011) 'Back to basics: The right to liberty and security of person and 'alternatives to detention' of refugees, asylum-seekers, stateless persons and other migrants', UNHCR Legal and Protection Policy Research Series, PPLA/2011/01.Rev 1 (online). Available from URL: www.refworld.org/docid/4dc935fd2.html (accessed 11 February 2019)

Einterz, E. M., Younge, O. and Hadi, C. (2018) 'The impact of a public health department's expansion from a one-step to a two-step refugee screening process on the detection and initiation of treatment of latent tuberculosis', *Public Health*, Vol. 159, pp. 27–30; doi: 10.1016/j.puhe.2018.03.008

European Parliament (2016) 'MEPs discuss fate of 10,000 refugee children' (online). Available from URL: www.europarl.europa.eu/pdfs/news/public/story/20160419STO23927/20160419STO23927_en.pdf (accessed 10 January 2018)

Faculty of Public Health (2016) 'Good public health practice framework 2016' (online). Available from URL: www.fph.org.uk/media/1304/good-public-health-practice-framework_-2016_final.pdf (accessed 10 October 2018)

Fainstein, S. (2010) *The Just City*, Ithaca, NY: Cornell University Press

Farrell, S., Wood, B., King-Andrews, H., Lougheed, D., Muckle, W., Burnett, L. and Turnbull, J. (2014) 'An examination of the delivery of psychiatric services within a shelter-based management of alcohol program for homeless adults', in Guirguis-Younger, M., McNeil, R. and Hwang, S. W. (eds) (2014) *Homelessness and Health in Canada*, Ottawa, University of Ottawa Press, pp. 255–74

Farrugia, D. and Gerrard, J. (2016) 'Academic knowledge and contemporary poverty: The politics of homelessness research', *Sociology*, Vol. 50, No. 2, pp. 267–84; doi: 10.1177/0038038514564436

Fassil, Y. (2000) 'Personal views: Looking after the health of refugees', *British Medical Journal*, Vol. 321, No. 7252, p. 59

Fazel, M., Wheeler, J. and Danesh, J. (2005) 'Prevalence of serious mental disorder in 7,000 refugees resettled in western countries: A systematic review', *The Lancet*, Vol. 365, No. 9467, pp. 1309–14; doi: 10.1016/S0140-6736(05)61027-6

Fazel, S., Geddes, J. and Kushel, M. (2014) 'The health of homeless people in high-income countries: Descriptive epidemiology, health consequences, and clinical and policy recommendations', *The Lancet*, Vol. 384, No. 9953, pp. 1529–40; doi: 10.1016/S0140-6736(14)61132-6

FEANTSA (2005) 'European typology of homelessness and housing exclusion' (online). Available from URL: www.feantsa.org/download/ethos2484215748748239888.pdf (accessed 28 March 2018)

FEANTSA and the Foundation Abbé Pierre (2018) 'Third overview of housing exclusion in Europe 2018' (online). Available from URL: www.feantsa.org/en/report/2018/03/21/the-second-overview-of-housing-exclusion-in-europe-2017?bcParent=27 (accessed 17 May 2018)

Felitti, V. J., Anda, R. F., Nordenberg, D., Williamson, D. F., Spitz, A. M., Edwards, V. and Marks, J. S. (1998) 'Relationship of childhood abuse and household dysfunction to many of the leading causes of death in adults: The Adverse

Childhood Experiences (ACE) study', *American Journal of Preventive Medicine*, Vol. 14, No. 4, pp. 245–58

Fenton, N. (2011) 'Deregulation or democracy? New media, news, neoliberalism and the public interest', *Continuum: Journal of Media & Cultural Studies*, Vol. 25, No. 1, pp. 63–72

Ferris, E. G. (2007) 'Abuse of power: Sexual exploitation of refugee women and girls', *Signs: Journal of Women in Culture and Society*, Vol. 32, No. 3, pp. 584–91; doi: 10.1086/510338

Filges, T., Montgomery, E. and Kastrup, M. (2016) 'The impact of detention on the health of asylum seekers: A systematic review', *Research on Social Work Practice*, Vol. 24; doi: 10.1177/1049731516630384

Fitzpatrick, S. (2005) 'Explaining homelessness: A critical realist perspective', *Housing, Theory and Society*, Vol. 22, No. 1, pp. 1–17

Fitzpatrick, S., Kemp, P. and Klinker, S. (2000) *Single Homelessness: An Overview of the Research in Britain*, Bristol: Policy Press

Fitzpatrick, S., Johnsen, S. and White, M. (2011a) 'Multiple exclusion homelessness in the UK: Key patterns and intersections', *Social Policy and Society*, Vol. 10, No. 4, pp. 501–12; doi: 10.1017/S147474641100025X

Fitzpatrick, S., Pawson, H., Bramley, G. and Wilcox, S. (2011b) 'The homelessness monitor: Tracking the impacts of policy and economic change in England 2011–2013 Year 1: Establishing the baseline' (online). Available from URL: www.crisis.org.uk/ending-homelessness/homelessness-knowledge-hub/homelessness-monitor/england/the-homelessness-monitor-england-2011 (accessed 10 July 2017)

Fitzpatrick, S., Johnsen, S. and Bramley, G. (2012) *Multiple Exclusion Homelessness in the UK: Migrants*, Briefing Paper No. 2. (Multiple Exclusion Homelessness in the UK: Briefing Papers), Edinburgh: Heriot-Watt University

Fitzpatrick, S., Bramley, G. and Johnsen, S. (2013) 'Pathways into multiple exclusion homelessness in seven UK cities', *Urban Studies*, Vol. 50, No. 1, pp. 148–68; doi: 10.1177/0042098012452329

Fitzpatrick, S., Bramley, G., Sosenko, F., Blenkinsopp, J., Wood, J., Johnsen, S., Littlewood, M. and Watts, B. (2018a) 'Destitution in the UK 2018' (online), Joseph Rowntree Foundation. Available from URL: www.jrf.org.uk/report/destitution-uk-2018 (accessed 12 September 2018)

Fitzpatrick, S., Pawson, H., Bramley, G., Wilcox, S., Watts, B. and Wood, J. (2018b) *The Homelessness Monitor: England*, York: Joseph Rowntree Foundation. Available from URL: www.crisis.org.uk/media/238700/homelessness_monitor_england_2018.pdf (accessed 17 July 2018)

Frameworks Institute (2017) 'Changing the conversation on social issues' (online). Available from URL: www.frameworksinstitute.org (accessed 2 June 2017)

Fraser, N. (2008). *Scales of Justice: Reimagining Political Space in a Globalizing World*, Cambridge Malden, MA: Polity Press

Gabrielatos, C. and Baker, P. (2008) 'Fleeing, sneaking, flooding: A corpus analysis of discursive constructions of refugees and asylum seekers in the UK press, 1996–2005', *Journal of English Linguistics*, Vol. 36, No. 1, pp. 5–38

Gaetz, S., O'Grady, B., Buccieri, K., Karabanow, J. and Marsolais, A. (2013) *Youth Homelessness in Canada: Implications for Policy and*

Practice, Toronto: Canadian Homelessness Research Network

Gagnon, A. J., Zimbeck, M. and Zeitlin, J. (2009) 'Migration to western industrialised countries and perinatal health: A systematic review', *Social Science & Medicine*, Vol. 69, No. 6, pp. 934–46

Garthwaite, K., Smith, K. E., Bambra, C. and Pearce, J. (2016) 'Desperately seeking reductions in health inequalities: Perspectives of UK researchers on past, present and future directions in health inequalities research', *Sociology of Health and Illness*, Vol. 38, No. 3, pp. 459–78

Geddie, E. (2009) 'Gender-based violence in Europe's fight against irregular migration', *Choices*, IPPF European Network. Available from URL: www.womenlobby.org/IMG/pdf/IPPF_interview_with_CDT_Nov_2009.pdf (accessed 28 March 2019)

Georgiadou, E., Morawa, E. and Erim, Y. (2017) 'High manifestations of mental distress in Arabic asylum seekers accommodated in collective centres for refugees in Germany', *International Journal of Environmental Research in Public Health*, Vol. 14, p. 612

Gerrard, J. and Farrugia, D. (2015) 'The "lamentable sight" of homelessness and the society of the spectacle', *Urban Studies*, Vol. 52, No. 12, pp. 2219–33; doi: 10.1177/0042098014542135

Gerritsen, A. A. M., Bramsen, I., Devillé, W., van Willigen, L. H. M., Hovens, J. E. and Vander Ploeg, H. M. (2006) 'Use of health care services by Afghan, Iranian, and Somali refugees and asylum seekers living in the Netherlands', *European Journal of Public Health*, Vol. 16, No. 4, pp. 394–9

Giddens, A. (1991) *Modernity and Self-Identity: Self and Society in the Late Modern Age*, Stanford, CA: Stanford University Press

Giddens, A. (2018) 'Globalization', in Iyall Smith, K. E. (ed.) (2018) *Sociology of Globalization: Cultures, Economies and Politics*, Abingdon: Routledge, pp. 19–26

Gillespie, M. (2012) *Trapped: Destitution and Asylum in Scotland*, Glasgow: Scottish Poverty Information Unit

Gilroy, P. (2004) *After Empire: Melancholy or Convivial Culture?*, London: Routledge

Glover V. and Barlow J. (2014) 'Psychological adversity in pregnancy: What works to improve outcomes?', *Journal of Children's Services*, vol. 9, No. 2. pp. 96–108; doi: 10.1108/JCS-01-2014-0003

Goering, P., Streiner, D., Adair, C., Aubry, T., Barker, J., Distasio, J., Hwang, S., Komaroff, J., Latimer, E., Somers, J. and Zabkiewicz, D. (2011) 'At home/chez soi trial protocol: A pragmatic, multi-site, randomised controlled trial of a Housing First intervention for homeless individuals with mental illness in five Canadian cities', *British Medical Journal Open*, Vol. 1, pp.e000323; doi: 10.1136/bmjopen-2011-000323

Goffman, E. (1967, rev. edn 2009) *Stigma: Notes on the Management of Spoiled Identity*, New York, NY: Simon and Schuster

Gowan, T. (2010) *Hobos, Hustlers, and Backsliders: Homeless in San Francisco*, Minneapolis, MN: University of Minnesota Press

Graham, L., Fischbacher, C. M., Stockton, D., Fraser, A., Fleming, M. and Greig, K. (2015) 'Understanding extreme mortality among prisoners: A national cohort study in Scotland using data linkage', *European Journal of Public Health,* Vol. 25, pp. 879–85; doi: 10.1093/eurpub/cku252

Greenfeld, P. (2018) 'Tented Britain: Rise in rough sleepers taking shelter under canvas', *Guardian.* Available from URL: www.theguardian.com/ society/2018/aug/10/tented-britain-rise-in-rough-sleepers-taking-shelter-under-canvas (accessed 11 February 2019)

Greenslade, R. (2005) *Seeking Scapegoats: The Coverage of Asylum in the UK Press,* London: Institute for Public Policy Research

Groot, S. and Hodgetts, D. (2015) 'The infamy of begging: A case-based approach to homelessness and radical commerce', *International Journal of Heritage Studies,* Vol. 23. No. 1, pp. 52–64; doi: 10.1080/14780887.2014.960984

Guardian (2018) ' "England seemed so close": Refugee, 15, crushed to death by Calais lorry' (online). Available from URL: www.theguardian.com/ world/2018/jan/16/england-seemed-so-close-refugee-15-crushed-to-death-by-calais-lorry (accessed 22 January 2018)

Guirguis-Younger, M. and McNeil, R. (2014) 'The development and operational context of an emergency shelter-based hospice in Ottawa, Ontario: A qualitative study', in Guirguis-Younger, M., McNeil, R. and Hwang, S. W. (eds) (2014) *Homelessness and Health in Canada,* Ottawa: University of Ottawa Press, pp. 293–312

Guirguis-Younger, M., McNeil, R. and Hwang, S. W. (2014) (eds) 'Introduction', in *Homelessness and Health in Canada,* Ottawa: University of Ottawa Press

Hall, S. M. (2015a) 'Focus: Migration and election 2015', *Discover Society,* Vol. 17. Available from URL: www.discoversociety.org/2015/02/01/focus-migration-and-election-2015 (accessed 11 February 2019)

Hall, S. M. (2015b) 'Migrant urbanisms: Ordinary cities and everyday resistance', *Sociology,* Vol. 49, No. 5, pp. 853–69; doi: 10.1177/0038038515586680

Hamilton, K. and Harris, J. (2009) *21 Days Later: Destitution and the Asylum System,* Glasgow: British Red Cross and Refugee Survival Trust

Hankivsky, O. (2012) 'Women's health, men's health, and gender and health: Implications of intersectionality', *Social Science & Medicine,* Vol. 74, No. 11, pp. 1712–20; doi: 10.1016/j.socscimed.2011.11.029

Harding, R. and Hamilton, P. (2009) 'Working girls: Abuse and choice in street level sex work? A study of homeless women in Nottingham', *British Journal of Social Work,* Vol. 39, No. 6, pp. 1118–37

Hermansson, A. C., Timpka, T. and Thyberg, M. (2003) 'The long-term impact of torture on the mental health of war-wounded refugees: Findings and implications for nursing programmes', *Scandinavian Journal of Caring Science,* Vol. 17, No. 4, pp. 317–24

Hetherington, K. and Hamlet, N. (2015) 'Restoring the public health response to homelessness in Scotland', Scottish Public Health Network report (online). Available from URL: www.scotphn.net/wp-content/uploads/2015/10/ Restoring-the-Public-Health-response-to-Homelessness-in-Scotland-May-2015.pdf (accessed 8 September 2016)

Hewett, N. and Halligan, A. (2010) 'Homelessness is a healthcare issue', *Journal of the Royal Society of Medicine,* Vol. 103, No. 8, pp. 306–7

Hewett, N., Halligan, A. and Boyce, T. (2012) 'A general practitioner and nurse led approach to improving hospital care for homeless people', *British Medical Journal*, Vol. 345, p. e5999; doi: 10.1136/bmj.e5999

Hewett, N., Buchman, P., Musariri, J., Sargeant, C., Johnson, P., Abeysekera, K., Grant, L., Oliver, E.a., Eleftheriades, C., Mccormick, B., Halligan, A., Marlin, N., Kerry, S. and Foster, G. R. (2016) 'Randomised controlled trial of GP-led in-hospital management of homeless people ("Pathway")', *Clinical Medicine*, Vol. 16, pp. 223–9; doi: 10.7861/clinmedicine.16-3-223

Heywood, A. (2011) *Global Politics*, Basingstoke: Palgrave Macmillan

Hodgetts, D, Hodgetts, A. and Radley, A. (2006) 'Life in the shadow of the media: Imaging street homelessness in London', *European Journal of Cultural Studies*, Vol. 9, No. 4, pp. 497–516

Hollander, A. C. (2013) 'Social inequalities in mental health and mortality among refugees and other immigrants to Sweden: Epidemiological studies of register data', *Global Health Action*, Vol. 6. Available from URL: www.ncbi.nlm.nih.gov/pmc/articles/PMC3696128 (accessed 14 February 2019)

Home Office (2007) *Enforcing the Rules: A Strategy To Ensure and Enforce Compliance With Our Immigration Laws*, London: Home Office

Homeless Link (2014) 'Investment needed to continue homeless hospital discharge improvement' (online). Available from URL: www.homeless.org.uk/connect/news/2015/feb/09/investment-needed-to-continue-homeless-hospital-discharge-improvement (accessed May 2017)

Homeless Link (2015) *The Unhealthy State of Homelessness: Health Audit Results*, London: Homeless Link

Homeless Link and St Mungo's (2012) 'Homeless Link and St Mungo's publish report on hospitals and the homeless' (online). Available from URL: www.gov.uk/government/news/homeless-link-and-st-mungo-s-publish-report-on-hospitals-and-the-homeless (accessed 10 January 2018)

Hutchinson, S., Page, A. and Sample, E. (2014) *Rebuilding Shattered Lives: The Final Report*, London: St Mungo's. Available from URL: www.mungos.org/publication/rebuilding-shattered-lives-final-report (accessed 24 November 2014)

Hwang, S. W. and Burns, T. (2014) 'Health interventions for people who are homeless', *The Lancet*, Vol. 384, No. 9953, pp. 1541–7

Hwang, S. W., Colantonio, A., Chiu, S., Tolomiczenko, G., Kiss, A., Cowan, L., Redelmeier, D. A. and Levinson, W. (2008) 'The effect of traumatic brain injury on the health of homeless people', *Canadian Medical Association Journal*, Vol. 179, No. 8, pp. 779–84

Hyde, J. (2005) 'From home to street: Understanding young people's transitions into homelessness', *Journal of Adolescence*, Vol. 28, pp. 171–83; doi: 10.1016/j.adolescence.2005.02.001

Immigration and Asylum Act (1999) 'Immigration and Asylum Act 1999' (online). Available from URL: www.legislation.gov.uk/ukpga/1999/33/contents (accessed 22 May 2005)

Institute of Health Equity (2015) 'The impact of adverse experiences in the home on the health of children and young people, and inequalities in prevalence and effects' (online). Available from URL: www.instituteofhealthequity.org/resources-reports/the-impact-of-adverse-experiences-in-the-home-on-children-and-young-people/impact-of-adverse-experiences-in-the-home.pdf

(accessed 10 October 2018)

ISD Scotland (2018) 'Health and social care data integration' (online). Available from URL: www.isdscotland.org/Health-Topics/Health-and-Social-Community-Care/Health-and-Social-Care-Integration (accessed 10 October 2018)

Jamieson, C. (2018) 'Uprooted and unprotected: The experiences of children forced into migration through northern France and a multi-agency approach to safeguarding them' (online). Available from URL: www.nspcc.org.uk/globalassets/documents/research-reports/uprooted-and-unprotected-ctac-report.pdf (accessed 11 February 2019)

JCHR (Joint Committee on Human Rights) (2007) *The Treatment of Asylum Seekers: Tenth Report of Session 2006–07* (online). London: House of Lords/House of Commons. Available from URL: www.publications.parliament.uk/pa/jt200607/jtselect/jtrights/81/81i.pdf (accessed 12 June 2015)

Johnsen, S. and Teixeira, L. (2012) ' "Doing it already?": Stakeholder perceptions of Housing First in the UK', *International Journal of Housing Policy*, Vol. 12, No. 2, pp. 183–203; doi: 10.1080/14616718.2012.681579

Johnsen, S., Cloke, P. and May, J. (2005) 'Transitory spaces of care: Serving homeless people on the street', *Health & Place*, Vol. 11, No. 4, pp. 323–35; doi: 10.1016/j.healthplace.2004.03.002

Johnsen, S., Fitzpatrick, S. and Watts, B. (2018) 'Homelessness and social control: A typology', *Housing Studies*, Vol. 33, No. 7, pp. 1106–26; doi: 10.1080/02673037.2017.1421912

Johnson, G. and Chamberlain, C. (2008) 'From youth to adult homelessness', *Australian Journal of Social Issues*, Vol. 43, No. 4, pp. 563–82

Johnson, G., Scutella, R., Tseng, Y. P. and Wood, G. (2015) *Entries and Exits from Homelessness: A Dynamic Analysis of the Relationship Between Structural Conditions and Individual Characteristics*, AHURI Final Report No. 248, Melbourne: Australian Housing and Urban Research Institute

Johnson, R. (2015) 'Editorial', *Housing, Care and Support*, Vol. 17, No. 3; doi: 10.1108/hcs-06-2014-0015

Kapilashrami, A., Hill, S. and Meer N. (2015) 'What can health inequalities researchers learn from an intersectionality perspective? Understanding social dynamics with an inter-sectional approach?', *Social Theory and Health*, Vol. 13, pp. 288–307; doi: 10.1057/sth.2015.16

Karabanow, J. and Kidd, S. (2014) 'Being young and homeless: Addressing youth homelessness from drop-in to drafting policy', in Guirguis-Younger, M., McNeil, R. and Hwang, S. W. (eds) *Homelessness and Health in Canada*, Ottawa, University of Ottawa Press, pp. 10–30

Kastrup, M. (2016) 'The impact of racism and discrimination on mental health of refugees and asylum seekers', *European Psychiatry*, Vol. 33, S43; doi: 10.1016/j.eurpsy.2016.01.896

Keller, A. S., Rosenfeld, B., Trinh-Shevrin, C., Meserve, C., Sachs, E., Leviss, J. A., Singer, E., Smith, H., Wilkinson, J., Kim, G., Allden, K. and Ford, D. (2003) 'Mental health of detained asylum seekers', *The Lancet*, Vol. 362, pp. 172123; doi: 10.1016/S0140-6736(03)14846-5

Kelly-Irving, M., Lepage, B., Dedieu, D., Bartley, M., Blane, D. and Grosclaude, P. (2013) 'Adverse childhood experiences and premature all-cause mortality',

European Journal of Epidemiology, Vol. 28, No. 9, pp. 721–34

Kendall, D.E. (2005) *Framing Class: Media Representations of Wealth and Poverty in America*, Lanham, MD: Rowman and Littlefield

Kennett, P., Forrest, R. and Marsh, A. (2013) 'The global economic crisis and the reshaping of housing opportunities', *Housing, Theory and Society*, Vol. 30, No. 1, pp. 10–28; doi: 10.1080/14036096.2012.683292

Kertesz, S., Crouch, K., Milby, J., Cusimano, R. and Schumacher, J. (2009) 'Housing First for homeless persons with active addiction: Are we over-reaching?', *The Milbank Quarterly*, Vol. 87, No. 2, pp. 495–534; doi: 10.1111/j.1468–0009.2009.00565.x

Kertesz, S., McNeil, G., Cash, W., Desmond, J., McGwin, J., Kelly, R. and Baggett, G. (2014) 'Unmet need for medical care and safety net accessibility among Birmingham's homeless', *Journal of Urban Health*, Vol. 91, No. 1, pp. 33–45; doi: 10.1007/s11524–013–9801–3

Khosravinik, M. (2009) 'The representation of refugees, asylum seekers and immigrants in British newspapers during the Balkan conflict (1999) and the British general election', *Discourse & Society*, Vol. 20, No. 4, pp. 477–98

Kidd, S. A. and Evans, J. D. (2010) 'Home is where you draw strength and rest: The meanings of home for houseless young people', *Youth Society*, Vol. 43, No. 2, pp. 752–73

Kim, M. M., Ford, J. D., Howard, D. L. and Bradford, D. W. (2010) 'Assessing trauma, substance abuse, and mental health in a sample of homeless men', *Health & Social Work*, Vol. 35, No. 1, pp. 39–48; doi: 10.1093/hsw/35.1.39

Kinsella, M. and Monk, C. (2009) 'Impact of maternal stress, depression & anxiety on fetal neurobehavioral development', *Clinical Obstetrics and Gynecology*, Vol. 52, No. 3, pp. 425–40; doi: 10.1097/GRF.0b013e3181b52df1

Kirkwood, S., Goodman, S., McVittie, C. and McKinlay, A. (2016) *The Language of Asylum: Refugees and Discourse*, Basingstoke: Palgrave Macmillan

Kontopantelis, E., Mamas, M. A., van Marwijk, H., Ryan, A. M., Buchan, I. E., Ashcroft, D. M. and Doran, T. (2018) 'Geographical epidemiology of health and overall deprivation in England, its changes and persistence from 2004 to 2015: A longitudinal spatial population study', *Journal of Epidemiology and Community Health*, Vol. 72, No. 2, pp. 140–7; doi: 10.1136/jech-2017-209999

Krusi, A., Small, W., Wood, E. and Kerr, T. (2009) 'An integrated supervised injecting program within a care facility for HIV-positive individuals: A qualitative evaluation', *AIDS Care*, Vol. 21, No. 5, pp. 638–44

Kusmer, K. (2002) *Down and Out and On the Road: The Homeless in American History*, New York, NY: Oxford University Press

Laing, R. D. (1965) *The Divided Self: An Existential Study in Sanity and Madness*, London: Pelican Press

Lancione, M. (2011) 'Homeless subjects and the chance of space: A more-than-human geography of homelessness in Turin' (Unpublished PhD), Durham: Durham University, Department of Geography

Langegger, S. and Koester, S. (2017) 'Moving on, finding shelter: The spatio-temporal camp', *International Sociology*, Vol. 32, No. 4, pp. 454–73; doi: 10.1177/0268580917701584

Last, J. M., Spasoff, R. A., Harris, S. S. and Thuriaux, M. C. (eds) (2001) *A Dictionary of Epidemiology*, New York, NY: Oxford University Press, 4th edn

Lebrun-Harris, L. A., Baggett, T. P., Jenkins, D. M., Sripipatana, A., Sharma, R., Hayashi, A. S., Daly, C. A. and Ngo-Metzger, Q. (2010) 'Health status and health care experiences among homeless patients in federally supported health centers: Findings from the 2009 patient survey', *Health Service Research*, Vol. 48, pp. 992–1017

Lewis, H. (2007) *Destitution in Leeds: The Experiences of People Seeking Asylum and Supporting Agencies*, York: Joseph Rowntree Charitable Trust. Available from URL: www.jrct.org.uk/userfiles/documents/Destitution%20in%20 Leeds%20(research%20report%20full).pdf (accessed 11 February 2019)

Lewis, H. and Waite, L. (2015) 'Asylum, immigration restrictions and exploitation: Hyperprecarity as a lens for understanding and tackling forced labour', *Anti-Trafficking Review*, Vol. 5; doi: 10.14197/atr.20121554

Lewis, H., Dwyer, P., Hodkinson, S. and Waite, L. (2014) 'Hyper-precarious lives: Migrants, work and forced labour in the Global North', *Progress in Human Geography*, Vol. 39, No. 5, pp. 580–600; doi: 10.1177/0309132514548303

Lind, R. A. and Danowski, J. A. (1999) 'The representation of the homeless in US electronic media: A computational linguistic analysis', in Min, E. (ed.) (1999) *Reading the Homeless: The Media's Image of Homeless Culture*, Westport, CT: Praeger, pp. 109–21

Littlewood, M., Bramley, G., Fitzpatrick, S. and Wood, J. (2017) *Eradicating 'Core Homelessness' in Scotland's Four Largest Cities: Providing an Evidence Base and Guiding a Funding Framework*, Edinburgh: Social Bite and iSPHERE, Heriot Watt University. Available from URL: http://social-bite.co.uk/wp-content/ uploads/2018/01/EradicatingCoreHomelessness.pdf (accessed February 2019)

Luchenski, S., Maguire, N., Aldridge, R. W., Hayward, A., Story, A., Perri, P., Withers, J., Clint, S., Fitzpatrick, S. and Hewett, N. (2017) 'What works in inclusion health: Overview of effective interventions for marginalised and excluded populations', *The Lancet*, Vol. 391, No. 10117; doi: 10.1016/ S0140-6736(17)31959-1

Lueck, K., Due, C. and Augoustinos, M. (2015) 'Neoliberalism and nationalism: Representations of asylum seekers in the Australian mainstream news media', *Discourse & Society*, Vol. 26, No. 5, pp. 608–29

McAdams, D. P. (1993) *The stories We Live By*, New York, NY: William Morrow

McAuley, A., Best, D., Taylor, A., Hunter, C. and Robertson, R. (2012) 'From evidence to policy: The Scottish national naloxone programme', *Drugs: Education, Prevention and Policy*, Vol. 19, No. 4, pp. 309–19; doi: 10.3109/09687637.2012.682232

McDonald, I. and Billings, P. (2007) 'The treatment of asylum seekers in the UK', *Social Welfare and Family Law*, Vol. 29, No. 2, pp. 49–65

McDonagh, T. (2011) *Tackling Homelessness and Exclusion: Understanding Complex Lives*, York: Joseph Rowntree Foundation. Available from URL: www.jrf.org. uk/sites/default/files/jrf/migrated/files/homelessness-exclusion-services-summary.pdf (accessed 13 April 2018)

McDonald, C. and Marston, G. (2005) 'Workfare as welfare: Governing unemployment in the advanced liberal state', *Critical Social Policy*, Vol. 25, No. 3, pp. 374–401

McGuinness, T. and Gower, M. (2017) *Briefing Paper: Immigration Detention in the UK: An Overview*, No. 7294, 13 June, London: House of Commons Library. Available from URL: http://researchbriefings.parliament.uk/ResearchBriefing/Summary/CBP-7294 (accessed 11 February 2019)

Mackenbach, J. P. (2011) 'Can we reduce health inequalities? An analysis of the English strategy (1997–2010)', *Journal of Epidemiology and Community Health*, Vol. 65, pp. 568–75

Mackenbach, J. P. (2016) 'The persistence of health inequalities in modern welfare states: The explanation of paradox', in Mackenbach, J. P. (ed.) (2016) *Health Inequalities in Europe. New Insights from Comparative Studies*, Rotterdam: Erasmus MC, pp. 179–92

McKendrick, J. H., Sinclair, S., Irwin, A., O'Donnell, H., Scott, G. and Dobbie, L. (2008) *The Media, Poverty and Public Opinion in the UK*, York: Joseph Rowntree Foundation

Mackie, P., Johnsen, S. and Wood, J. (2017) *Ending Rough Sleeping: What Works? An International Evidence Review*, London: Crisis. Available from URL: www.crisis.org.uk/ending-homelessness/homelessness-knowledge-hub/services-and-interventions/ending-rough-sleeping-what-works-an-international-evidence-review (accessed 12 September 2018)

Macleod, J., Copeland, L., Hickman, M., McKenzie, J., Kimber, J., De Angelis, D. and Robertson, R. (2010) 'The Edinburgh addiction cohort: Recruitment and follow-up of a primary care based sample of injection drug users and non drug-injecting controls', *BMC Public Health*, Vol. 10, p. 101; doi: 10.1186/1471-2458-10-101

McNeil, R. and Guirguis-Younger, M. (2014) 'Dignity in design: The siting and design of community and shelter-based health facilities for homeless persons', in Guirguis-Younger, M., McNeil, R. and Hwang, S. W. (eds) (2014) *Homelessness and Health in Canada*, Ottawa, University of Ottawa Press, pp. 233–54

McNeil, R., Guirguis-Younger, M., Dilley, L. B., Aubry, T. D., Turnbull, J. and Hwang, S. W. (2012) 'Harm reduction services as a point-of-entry to and source of end-of-life care and support for homeless and marginally housed persons who use alcohol and/or illicit drugs: A qualitative analysis', *BMC Public Health*, Vol. 12, No. 1, p. 312

McNoughton, C. and Sanders, T. (2007) 'Housing and transitional phases of "disordered" lives: The case of leaving homelessness and street work', *Housing Studies*, Vol. 22, No. 6, pp. 885–900

McQuail, D. (2005) *McQuail's Mass Communication Theory*, 5th edn, Thousand Oaks, CA: Sage

Magat, I. (1999) 'Israeli and Japanese immigrants to Canada: Home, belonging, and the territorialization of identity', *Ethos*, Vol. 27, No. 2, pp. 119–144

Mallett, S. (2004) 'Understanding home: A critical review of the literature', *The Sociological Review*, Vol. 52, No. 1, pp. 62–89

Mallett, S., Rosenthal, D., Keys, D. and Averill, R. (2010) *Moving Out: Moving On. Young People's Pathways In and Through Homelessness*, Abingdon: Routledge

Marmot, M. (2010) *Strategic review of health inequalities in England post-2010*.

Marmot review final report. London, University College London

Marmot, M. (2015a) *The Health Gap: The Challenge of an Unequal World,* London: Bloomsbury

Marmot, M. (2015b) *Status Syndrome: How Your Place on the Social Gradient Directly Affects Your Health,* London: Bloomsbury

Marmot, M. (2017a) 'Inclusion health: Addressing the causes of the causes', *The Lancet,* Vol. 391, No. 10117, pp. 186–8; doi: 10.1016/S0140-6736(17)32848-9

Marmot, M. (2017b) 'NCDs, health equity and the social determinants of health', remarks in opening expert plenary session at NCD conference in Montevideo, 18 October 2017. Available from URL: https://marmot-review.blogspot.com/2017/11/ncds-health-equity-and-social.html (accessed 17 March 2019)

Marshall, B. D. L. and Kerr, T. (2015) 'Housing and HIV/AIDS among people who inject drugs: public health evidence for effective policy response', in Zukin, S., Kasinitz, P. and Chen, X. (eds) (2015) *Global Cities, Local Streets,* New York, NY: Routledge, pp. 135–53

Marshall, T. (2018) *Divided: Why We're Living in an Age of Walls,* London: Elliott and Thompson

Maternity Action (2018) 'What price safe motherhood? Charging for NHS maternity care in England and its impact on migrant women' (online). Available from URL: www.maternityaction.org.uk/policy/publications/what-price-safe-motherhood-charging-for-nhs-maternity-care-in-england-and-its-impact-on-migrant-women (accessed 23 September 2018)

May, J., Cloke, P. and Johnsen, S. (2007) 'Alternative cartographies of homelessness: Rendering visible British women's experiences', *Gender, Place & Culture,* Vol. 14, No. 2, pp. 121–41

Mayberry, M. (2013) 'Gay-straight alliances: Youth empowerment and working toward reducing stigma of LGBT youth', *Humanity & Society,* Vol. 37, No. 1, pp. 35–54; doi: 0.1177/0160597612454358

Mayock, P. and Sheridan, S. (2012) *Women's 'Journeys' to Homelessness: Key Findings from a Biographical Study of Homeless Women in Ireland,* Women and Homelessness in Ireland, Research Paper No. 1, Dublin: School of Social Work and Social Policy and Children's Research Centre, Trinity College Dublin

MEAM (Making Every Adult Matter) (2009) *A Four-Point Manifesto for Tackling Multiple Needs and Exclusions,* London: MEAM

Mitchell, D. (1997) 'The annihilation of space by law: The roots and implications of anti-homeless laws in the United States', *Antipode,* Vol. 29, pp. 303–36

Mitchell, D. (2003) *The Right to the City: Social Justice and the Fight for Public Space,* London: Guildford Press

Monbiot, G. (2015) 'Skivers and strivers: This 200-year-old myth won't die', *The Guardian.* Available from URL: www.theguardian.com/commentisfree/2015/jun/23/skivers-strivers-200-year-old-myth-wont-die (accessed 11 February 2019)

Montgomery E. (2011) 'Trauma, exile and mental health in young refugees', *Acta Psychiatry Scandinavica,* Vol. 124, pp. 1–46

Morris, A., Judd, B. and Kavanagh, K. (2005) 'Marginality amidst plenty: Pathways into homelessness for older Australians', *Australian Journal of Social Issues*, Vol. 40, No. 2, pp. 241–51; doi: 10.1002/j.1839-4655.2005.tb00969.x

Morrison, D. S. (2009) 'Homelessness as an independent risk factor for mortality: Results from a retrospective cohort study', *International Journal of Epidemiology*, Vol. 38, No. 3, pp. 877–83; doi: 10.1016/j.aip. 2012.08.002

Moxley, D. P., Washington, O. G. and Calligan, H. F. (2012) 'Narrative insight into risk, vulnerability and resilience among older homeless African American women', *The Arts in Psychotherapy*, Vol. 39, No. 5, pp. 471–8

Murphy, S. (2009) ' "Compassionate strategies" of managing homelessness: Postrevanchist geographies in San Francisco'. *Antipode*, Vol. 41, No. 2, pp. 305–25

Mutere, M., Nyamathi, A., Christiani, A., Sweat, J., Avila, G. and Hobaica, L. (2014) 'Homeless youth seeking health and life-meaning through popular culture and the arts', *Child and Youth Services*, Vol. 35, No. 3, pp. 273–87; doi: 10.1080/0145935X.2014.950416

National Records of Scotland (2018) 'Drug related deaths in Scotland 2017' (online). Available from URL: www.nrscotland.gov.uk/files//statistics/drug-related-deaths/17/drug-related-deaths-17-pub.pdf (accessed 22 July 208)

National Statistics for Scotland (2018) 'Homelessness in Scotland: 2017 to 2018' (online). Available from URL: www.gov.scot/publications/homelessness-scotland-2017–18/pages/1 (accessed 17 September 2018)

Naysmith, S. (2016) 'Health boards told to fill £15 million cuts in funding for drugs and alcohol care', *The Herald*. Available from URL: www.heraldscotland.com/news/14241634.Health_boards_told_to_fill___15_million_cut_in_funding_for_drug_and_alcohol_care (accessed 2 June 2017)

NHS Health Scotland (2016a) 'Human rights and the right to health' (online). Available from URL: www.healthscotland.scot/media/1276/human-rights-and-the-right-to-health_dec2016_english.pdf (accessed 10 December 2017)

NHS Health Scotland (2016b) 'Health and homelessness' (online). Available from URL: www.healthscotland.scot/media/1251/health-and-homelessness_nov2016_english.pdf (accessed 6 June 2017)

NHS Scotland (2001) *Health and Homelessness Guidance*, Edinburgh: Scottish Executive. Available from URL: www.sehd.scot.nhs.uk/publications/hahg/hahg.pdf (accessed 10 October 2018)

Nicholls, S. (2018) 'Hungarian MP proposes law to make homelessness unconstitutional', *Euronews*, 13 August. Available from URL: www.euronews.com/2018/06/13/hungarian-mp-proposes-to-make-homelessness-unconstitutional (accessed 27 August 2018)

Nielsen, S. F., Hjorthøj, C. R., Erlangsen, A. and Nordentoft, M. (2011) 'Psychiatric disorders and mortality among people in homeless shelters in Denmark: A nationwide register-based cohort study', *The Lancet*, Vol. 377, pp. 2205–14; doi: 10.1016/S0140-6736(11)60747-2

O'Docherty, K. and Lecouteur, A. (2007) 'Asylum seekers, boat people and illegal immigrants: Social categorization in the media', *Australian Journal of Psychology*, Vol. 59, No. 1, pp. 1–12

OECD (2015) 'In it together: Why inequality benefits all' (online). Available from URL: www.oecd.org/social/in-it-together-why-less-inequality-benefits-all-

9789264235120-en.htm (accessed 10 May 2018)

OECD (2017) 'Data: poverty rates' (online). Available from URL: https://data. oecd.org/inequality/poverty-rate.htm (accessed 10 May 2018)

Ogunsiji, O., Wilkes, L., Jackson, D. and Peters, K. (2012) 'Suffering and smiling: West African immigrant women's experience of intimate partner violence', *Journal of Clinical Nursing*, Vol. 21, Nos 11–12, pp. 1659–65; doi: 10.1111/j.1365–2702.2011.03947.x

O'Neill, M. (2010) *Asylum, Migration and Community*, Bristol: Policy Press

O'Neill, M. and Hubbard, P. (2012) 'Asylum, exclusion, and the social role of arts and culture', *Moving Worlds: A Journal of Transcultural Writings*, Vol. 12, No. 2, pp. 46–82. Available from URL: www.movingworlds.net/volumes/12/asylum-accounts (accessed 4 June 2016)

O'Neill, M., Gerstein Pineau, M., Kendall-Taylor, N., Volmert, D. and Stevens, A. (2016) *Finding a Better Frame: How To Create More Effective Messages on Homelessness in the United Kingdom. A Strategic Report*, London: Crisis and Frame Works Institute

O'Toole, T. P., Buckel, L., Bourgault, C., Blumen, J., Redlhan, S. G., Jiang, L. and Friedmann, P. (2010) 'Applying the chronic care model to homeless veterans: Effect of a population approach to primary care on utilization and clinical outcomes', *American Journal of Public Health*, Vol. 100, No. 12, pp. 2493–9

Oxfam (2015) 'Inequality and the end of extreme poverty' (online). Available from URL: https://policy-practice.oxfam.org.uk/publications/inequality-and-the-end-of-extreme-poverty-577506 (accessed 12 March 2018)

Oxfam (2017) 'An economy for the 99%' (online). Available from URL: www. oxfam.org/en/research/economy-99 (accessed 7 June 2018)

Oxford Analytica (2016) 'Daily brief service Greece: Refugee reception could break down in October', 12 September. Available from URL: https://daily-brief.oxan.com/Analysis/DB213492/Greek-refugee-reception-could-break-down-in-October (accessed 8 September 2018)

Padgett, D. (2007) 'There's no place like (a) home: Ontological security among persons with serious mental illness in the United States', *Social Science & Medicine*, Vol. 64, pp. 1925–36; doi: 10.1016/j.socscimed.2007.02.011

Padgett, D. K., Gulcur, L. and Tsemberis, S. (2006) 'Housing first services for people who are homeless with co-occurring serious mental illness and substance abuse', *Research on social work practice*, Vol. 16, No. 1, pp. 74–83; doi: 10.1177/1049731505282593

Padgett, D. K., Stanhope, V., Henwood, B. F. and Stefancic, A. (2011) 'Substance use outcomes among homeless clients with serious mental illness: Comparing housing first with treatment first programs', *Community Mental Health Journal*, Vol. 47, No. 2, pp. 227–32

Page, M. (2017) 'Forgotten youth: Homeless LGBT youth of color and the Runaway and Homeless Youth Act', *Northwestern Journal of Law & Social Policy*, Vol. 12, No. 2, pp. 17–45

Parker, S. (2015) ' "Unwanted invaders": The representation of refugees and asylum seekers in the UK and Australian print media', *eSharp*, Vol. 23. Available from URL: www.gla.ac.uk/media/media_404384_en.pdf (accessed 11 February 2019)

Parsell, C. (2010) 'Homeless is what I am, not who I am': Insights From an Inner-city Brisbane Study, *Urban Policy and Research*, Vol. 28, No. 2, pp. 181–194; doi: 10.1080/08111141003793966

Parsell, C. (2011) 'Homeless identitiesE enacted and ascribed', *British Journal of Sociology*, Vol. 62, No. 3, pp. 442–61; doi: 10.1111/j.1468–4446.2011.01373.x

Pathway (2017) *Primary Care*, London: Pathway. Available from URL: www.pathway.org.uk (accessed 12 May 2018)

Pauly, B. (2014) 'Close to the street:Nnursing practice with people marginalized by homelessness and substance use', in Guirguis-Younger, M., McNeil, R. and Hwang, S. W. (eds) (2014) *Homelessness and Health in Canada*, Ottawa: University of Ottawa Press, pp. 211–32

Pearson, C., Montgomery, A. E. and Locke, G. (2009) 'Housing stability among homeless individuals with serious mental illness participating in housing first programs', *Journal of Community Psychology*, Vol. 37, No. 3, pp. 404–17; doi: 10.1002/jcop. 20303

Peck, J. and Tickell, A. (2002) Neoliberalising space. In: Brenner, N and Theodore, N (eds) *Spaces of Neoliberalism: Urban Restructuring in North America and Western Europe*. Oxford: Blackwell, pp. 33–57

Percac-Lima, S., Ashburner, J., Bond, M., Oo, B. and Atlas, S. (2013) 'Decreasing disparities in breast cancer screening in refugee women using culturally tailored patient navigation', *Journal of General Internal Medicine*, Vol. 28, No. 11, p. 1463; doi: 10.1007/s11606–013–2491–4

Perkowski, N. (2016) 'Deaths, interventions, humanitarianism and human rights in the Mediterranean "migration crisis" ', *Mediterranean Politics*, Vol. 21, No. 2, pp. 331–5; doi: 10.1080/13629395.2016.1145827

Pettitt, J. (2013) *The Poverty Barrier: The Right to Rehabilitation for Survivors of Torture in the UK*. London: Freedom from Torture. Available from URL: www.freedomfromtorture.org/sites/default/files/documents/Poverty%20 report%20FINAL%2 0a4%20web.pdf (accessed 11 February 2019)

Phillimore, J. (2015) 'Delivering maternity services in an era of superdiversity: The challenges of novelty and newness', *Ethnic and Racial Studies*, Vol. 38, No. 4, pp. 568–82; doi: 10.1080/01419870.2015.980288

Phillimore, J., Ergun, E., Goodson, L. and Hennessy, D. (2007) *They Do Not Understand the Problem I Have: Refugee Well-Being and Mental Healt,*. York: Joseph Rowntree Foundation

Piat, M., Polvere, L., Kirst, M., Voronka, J., Zabkiewicz, D., Plante, M. C., Isaak, C., Nolin, D., Nelson, G. and Goering, P. (2015) 'Pathways into homelessness: Understanding how both individual and structural factors contribute to and sustain homelessness in Canada', *Urban Studies*, Vol. 52, No. 13, pp. 2366–82

Pickering, S. (2001) 'Common sense and original deviancy: News discourses and asylum seekers in Australia', *Journal of Refugee Studies*, Vol. 14, No. 2, pp. 169–86; doi: 10.1093/jrs/14.2.169

Pickett, K. and Pearl, M. (2001) 'Multilevel analyses of neighbourhood socioeconomic socioeconomic context and health outcomes: A critical review', *Journal of Epidemiology and Community Health*, Vol. 55, No. 2, pp. 111–22

Pickett, K., and Wilkinson, R. (2010) *The Spirit Level*, London: Penguin

Pineteh, E. (2005) 'Memories of home and exile: Narratives of Cameroonian asylum seekers in Johannesburg', *Journal of Intercultural Studies*, Vol. 26, No. 4, pp. 379–99

Pleace, N. (1998) 'Single homelessness and social exclusion: The unique and the extreme', *Social Policy and Administration*, Vol. 32, No. 1, pp. 46–59; doi: 10.1111/1467–9515.00085

Pleace, N. (2008) *Effective Services for Substance Misuse and Homelessness in Scotland: Evidence from an International Review*, Edinburgh: Scottish Government

Pleace, N. (2017) 'The action plan for preventing homelessness in Finland: 2016–2019: The culmination of an integrated strategy to end homelessness?', *European Journal of Homelessness*, Vol. 11, No. 2, pp. 95–115

Popescu, G. (2016) 'The effect of mandatory prolonged detention on the mental health of asylum seekers and refugees', *American Journal of Medical Research*, Vol. 3, No. 2, p. 188

Prior, J. (2006) *Destitute and Desperate: A Report on the Numbers of 'Failed' Asylum Seekers in Newcastle upon Tyne and the Services Available to Them*, Newcastle: Open Door

Public Bodies (Joint Working) (Scotland) Act (2014) 'Public Bodies (Joint Working)(Scotland) Act 2014' (online). Available from URL: www.legislation.gov.uk/asp/2014/9/contents/enacted (accessed 10 October 2018)

Public Health England (2016) 'Longer lives – healthier lives' (online). Available from URL: https://fingertips.phe.org.uk/profile/mortality-profile/data#page/0 (accessed 18 July 2017)

Rankin, K., Kamizaki, K. and McLean, H. (2015) 'Toronto's changing neighbourhoods: Gentrification of shopping streets', in Zukin, S., Kasinitz, P. and Chen, X. (eds) (2015) *Global Cities, Local Streets*, New York, NY: Routledge, Chapter 6

Rapoport, A. (2000) 'Theory, housing and culture', *Housing, Theory and Society*, Vol. 17, No. 4, pp. 145–65; doi: 10.1080/140360900300108573

Råssjö, E. B., Byrskog, U., Samir, R., Klingberg-Allvin, M. (2013) 'Somali women's use of maternity health services and the outcome of their pregnancies: A descriptive study comparing Somali immigrants with native-born Swedish women', *Sexual and Reproductive Health*, Vol. 4, No. 3, pp. 99–106; doi: 10.1016/j.srhc.2013.06.001

Ravenhill, M. (2014) *The Culture of Homelessness*, Abingdon: Routledge

Raworth, K. (2017) *Doughnut Economics: Seven Ways to Think Like a 21st-Century Economist*, Chelsea, VT: Chelsea Green Publishing

Ream, G. L. and Forge, N. R. (2014) 'Homeless lesbian, gay, bisexual, and transgender (LGBT) youth in New York City: Insights from the field', *Child Welfare*, Vol. 93, No. 2, pp. 7–22

Redman, E. A., Reay, H. J., Jones, L., Roberts, R. J. (2011) 'Self-reported health problems of asylum seekers and their understanding of the national health service: A pilot study', *Public Health*, Vol. 125, No. 3, pp. 142–4; doi: 10.1016/j.puhe.2010.10.002

Reed, R. V., Fazel, M., Jones, L., Panter-Brick, C. and Stein, A. (2012) 'Mental health of displaced and refugee children resettled in low-income and middle-income countries: Risk and protective factors', *The Lancet*, Vol. 379, No. 9812, pp. 250–65

Rees, S. and Pease, B. (2007) 'Domestic violence in refugee families in Australia: Rethinking settlement policy and practice', *Journal of Immigrant and Refugee Studies*, Vol. 5, No. 2, pp. 1–19; doi: 10.1300/J500v05n02_01

Reeve, K., Casey, R. and Goudie, R. (2006) *Homeless Women: Still Being Failed Yet Striving To Survive*, London: Crisis. Available from URL: www4.shu.ac.uk/research/cresr/sites/shu.ac.uk/files/homeless-women-striving-survive.pdf (accessed 6 January 2017)

Reeve, K., Casey, R. and Goudie, R. (2007) *Homelessness Careers, Homelessness Landscapes*, London: Crisis

Refugee Action (2006) *The Destitution Trap: Research into Destitution Among Refused Asylum Seekers in the UK*, London: Refugee Action

Refugee Council (2018) 'Asylum statistices annual trends February 2018' (online). Available from URL: www.refugeecouncil.org.uk/assets/0004/2566/Asylum_Statistics_Annual_Trends_Feb_2018.pdf (accessed 12 October 2018)

Reimer-Kirkham, S. and Sharma, S. (2011) 'Adding religion to gender, race, and class: Seeking new insights on intersectionality in health care contexts', in Hankivsky, O. (ed.) (2011) *Health Inequities in Canada: Intersectional Frameworks and Practices*, Vancouver: University of British Columbia Press, pp. 112–31

Renedo, A. and Jovchelovitch, S. (2007) 'Expert knowledge, cognitive polyphasia and health: A study on social representations of homelessness among professionals working in the voluntary sector in London', *Journal of Health Psychology*, Vol. 12, No. 5, pp. 779–90; doi: 10.1177/1359105307080611

Robertson, J. (2017) 'Misadventure in Muirhouse. HIV infection: A modern plague and persisting public health problem', *Journal of the Royal College of Physicians of Edinburgh*, Vol. 27, pp. 88–93; doi: 10.4997/JRCPe.2017.119

Robjant, K., Hassan, R. and Katona, C. (2009a) 'Mental health implications of detaining asylum seekers: A systematic review', *British Journal of Psychiatry*, Vol. 194, pp. 306–12; doi: 10.1192/bjp.bp. 108.053223

Robjant, K., Robbins, I. and Senior, V. (2009b) 'Psychological distress amongst immigration detainees: A cross-sectional questionnaire study', *British Journal of Clinical Psychology*, Vol. 48, pp. 275–86; doi: 10.1348/014466508X397007

Roche, M. (2004) 'Complicated problems, complicated solutions? Homelessness and joined-up policy responses', *Social Policy & Administration*, Vol. 38, No. 7, pp. 758–74; doi: 10.1111/j.1467–9515.2004.00417.x

Roche, M. A., Duffield, C., Smith, J., Kelly, D., Cooke, R., Bichel-Findlay, J., Saunders, C. and Carter, D. J. (2018) 'Nurse-led primary health care for homeless men: A multimethods descriptive study', *International Nursing Review*, Vol. 65, No. 3, pp. 392–9; doi: 10.1111/inr.12419

Rosa, E. (2016) 'Discrete practices of resistance by Roma migrants in Turin and Marseille', *Cultures & Conflits*, Vol. 101, No. 1, pp. 19–34

Rosano, A. (2018) *Access to Primary Care and Preventative Health Services of Migrants*, Springer Briefs in Public Health, New York, NY: Springer

Rose, N. (1991) 'Governing "advanced" liberal democracies', in Barry, A., Osborne, T. and Rose, N. (eds) *Foucault and Political Reason: Liberalism, Neo-Liberalism, and Rationalities of* Governmen,. Chicago, IL: University of Chicago Press, pp. 37–64

Rose, N. (1999) *Governing the Soul: The Shaping of the Private Sel,*. London: Free Association Books

Rosello, M. (2012) 'Refugee aesthetics: Agency and storytelling in Chris Cleve's *The other hand and Femde Haut'*, *Moving Worlds*, Vol. 12, No. 2, pp. 5–15

Rosenblum, A., Magura, S., Fong, C., Curry, P., Norwood, C. and Casella, D. (2006) 'Effects of peer mentoring on HIV-affected youths' substance use risk and association with substance using friends', *Journal of Social Service Research*, Vol. 32, No. 2, pp. 45–60; doi: 10.1300/J079v32n02_03

Ruddick, S. (1996) *Young and Homeless in Hollywood*, London: Routledge

Safety4Sisters (2016) 'Migrant women's rights to safety pilot project 2016' (online). Available from URL: www.southallblacksisters.org.uk/wp-content/uploads/2016/11/Safety4Sisters-North-West-Report.pdf (accessed 28 February 2017)

Said, E. (1979) *Orientalism: Western Representations of the Orient*, New York, NY: Pantheon

Sanchez, M. (2018) 'Venezuelan refugees feel unwanted in Peru', *Aljazera*. Available from URL: www.aljazeera.com/news/2018/09/venezuela-refugees-feel-unwanted-peru-180901130120884.html (accessed 24 September 2018)

Sassen, S. (2011) *The Global City: New York, London, Tokyo*, Princeton NJ: Princeton University Press

Sassen, S. (2012) *Cities in a World Economy*, Los Angeles, CA: Sage

Saunders, P. and Williams, P. (1988) 'The constitution of the home: Towards a research agenda', *Housing Studies*, Vol. 32, No. 32, pp. 81–93; doi: 10.1080/02673038808720618

Savage, T. (ed.) (2009) *Profiling London's Rough Sleepers: A Longitudinal Analysis of CHAIN Data*, London: St Mungo's. Available from URL: www.mungos.org/wp-content/uploads/2017/07/Profiling-Londons-Rough-Sleepers-A-Longitudinal-Analysis-of-CHAIN-Data.pdf?x74044 (accessed 10 May 2011)

Schneider, J. (2007) *Better Outcomes for the Most Excluded*, Nottingham: University of Nottingham and Nottinghamshire Healthcare Trust

Schrecker, T. and Bambra, C. (2015) *How Politics Makes Us Sick: Neoliberal Epidemics*, London: Springer

Schwartz, D. R., Hames, C. A., Wagner, A. C. and Hart, T. A. (2014) 'Sexual risk behaviours and sexual health outcomes in Canada', in Guirguis-Younger, M., McNeil, R. and Hwang, S. W. (eds) (2014) *Homelessness and Health in Canada*, Ottawa, University of Ottawa Press, pp. 14–35

Scott, S., Curnock, E., Mitchell, R., Robinson, M., Taulbut, M., Tod, E. and McCartney, G. (2013) *What Would It Take To Eradicate Health Inequalities? Testing the Fundamental Causes Theory of Health Inequalities in Scotland*, Glasgow: NHS Health Scotland

Scottish Executive (2005) 'Health and homelessness standards' (online). Available from URL: www.gov.scot/Resource/Doc/37428/0012622.pdf (accessed 10 October 2018)

Scottish Government (2005) 'Code of guidance on homelessness' (online). Available from URL: https://beta.gov.scot/publications/code-guidance-homelessness (accessed 10 October 2018)

Scottish Government (2009) 'Prevention of homelessness guidance' (online). Available from URL: https://beta.gov.scot/publications/prevention-homelessness-guidance (accessed 10 October 2018)

Scottish Government (2015) 'Housing advice note' (online). Available from URL: www.gov.scot/resource/0048/00484861.pdf (accessed 10 October 2018)

Scottish Government (2016a) *Scottish House Condition Survey 2015: Key Findings*, Edinburgh: Scottish Government

Scottish Government (2016b) *Housing Options Guidance*, Edinburgh: Scottish Government and COSLA. Available from URL: www.gov.scot/Resource/0049/00494940.pdf (accessed 23 June 2018)

Scottish Government (2016c) 'Policy: Homelessness' (online). Available from URL: https://beta.gov.scot/policies/homelessness (accessed 10 October 2018)

Scottish Government (2017) 'Homeless and Rough Sleepers Action Group' (online). Available from URL: https://beta.gov.scot/groups/homelessness-and-rough-sleeping-action-group (accessed 10 October 2018)

Scottish Government (2018a) 'Ending homelessness: The report on the final recommendations of the Homeless and Rough Sleeping Action Group' (online). Available from URL: www.gov.scot/binaries/content/documents/govscot/publications/factsheet/2018/06/homelessness-and-rough-sleeping-action-group-final-report/documents/c98c5965-cabf-4933–9aae-26d9ff8f0d12/c98c5965-cabf-4933–9aae-26d9ff8f0d12/govscot%3Adocument (accessed 30 November 2018)

Scottish Government (2018b) 'Minimum unit pricing' (online). Available from URL: www.gov.scot/Topics/Health/Services/Alcohol/minimum-pricing (accessed 23 July 2018)

Scottish Government (2018c) 'Public health priorities for Scotland' (online). Available from URL: www.gov.scot/Resource/0053/00536757.pdf (accessed 10 October 2018)

Scottish Government (2018d) 'Homelessness in Scotland: 2017 to 2018' (online). Available from URL: www.gov.scot/publications/homelessness-scotland-2017–18/pages/4 (accessed 10 October 2018)

Scottish Government (2018e) 'Homelessness Prevention Strategy Group' (online). Available from URL: https://beta.gov.scot/groups/homelessness-prevention-and-strategy-group (accessed 10 October 2018)

Scottish Government (n.d.) 'Health and homelessness group' (online). Available from URL: https://beta.gov.scot/groups/health-and-homelessness-group (accessed 10 October 2018)

Scottish Housing Register (2014) 'Housing options in Scotland: A thematic enquiry' (online). Available from URL: www.scottishhousingregulator.gov.uk/sites/default/files/publications/Housing%20Options%20Report%20-%20Web%20Version.pdf (accessed 11 February 2019)

Scottish Prison Service (2017) 'SHORE standards' (online). Available from URL: www.sps.gov.uk/Corporate/Publications/Publication-5363.aspx (accessed 10 October 2018)

Semenza, J. C., Carrillo-Santisteve, P., Zeller, H., SandgrenMarieke, A., van der

Werf, J., Severi, E., Pastore Celentano, L., Wiltshire, E., Suk, J. E., Dinca, I., Noori, T. and Kramarz, P. (2016) 'Public health needs of migrants, refugees and asylum seekers in Europe, 2015: Infectious disease aspects', *European Journal of Public Health*, Vol. 26, No. 3, pp. 372–373; doi: 10.1093/eurpub/ckw023

Sen, P. (2016) 'The mental health needs of asylum seekers and refugees – challenges and solutions', *British Journal of Psychology International*, Vol. 13, No. 2, pp. 30–2

Sermons, M. W. and Henry, M. (2010) *Demographics of Homelessness Series: The Rising Elderly Population*, Washington, DC: Homelessness Research Institute

Shannon, P. J., Vinson, G. A., Wieling, E., Cook, T. and Letts, J. (2015) 'Torture, war trauma, and mental health symptoms of newly arrived Karen refugees', *Journal of Loss and Trauma*, Vol. 20, No. 6, pp. 577–90; doi: 10.1080/15325024.2014.965971

Sheldrick, G. (2014)' It's good but I don't like the food says asylum seekers: 130 migrants move to top hotel', *Daily Express*, 14 September. Available at URL: www.express.co.uk/news/uk/514893/130-asylum-seekers-seaside-hotel (accessed 10 June 2018)

Shelton, K. H., Taylor, P. J., Bonner, A. and van den Bree, M. (2009) 'Risk factors for homelessness: Evidence from a population-based study', *Psychiatric Services*, Vol. 60, No. 4, pp. 465–72

Sherwood, H. (2018) 'Windsor council leader calls for removal of homeless before royal wedding' , *The Guardian*. Available from URL: www.theguardian.com/society/2018/jan/03/windsor-council-calls-removal-homeless-people-before-royal-wedding (accessed 10 May 2018)

Shields, T. G. (2001) 'Network news construction of homelessness: 1980–1993', *Communication Review*, Vol. 4, No. 2, pp. 193–218

Shorter, G., Heather, N., Bray, J. W., Giles, E. L., Holloway, A., Barbosa, C., Berman, A. H., O'Donnell, A. J., Clarke, M., Stockdale, K. J. and Newbury-Birch, D. (2017) 'The "Outcome Reporting in Brief Intervention Trials: Alcohol" (ORBITAL) framework: Protocol to determine a core outcome set for efficacy and effectiveness trials of alcohol screening and brief intervention', *Trials*, Vol. 18, No. 611, pp. 1–7; doi: 10.1186/s13063-017-2335-3

Shortt, N. K., Rhynas, S. and Holloway, A. (2017) 'Place and recovery from alcohol dependence: A journey through photovoice', *Health & Place*, Vol. 47, pp. 147–53; doi: 10.1016/j.healthplace.2017.08.008

Small, R., Gagnon, A., Gissler, M., Zeitlin, J., Bennis, M. and Glazier, R. (2009) 'Somali women and their pregnancy outcomes postmigration: Data from six receiving countries', *International Journal of Obstetrics of Gynecology*, Vol. 115, No. 3, pp. 1630–40; doi: 10.1111/j.1471-0528.2008.01942.x

Smith, N. (2001) 'Global social cleansing: Postliberal revanchism and the export of zero tolerance', *Social Justice*, Vol. 28, No. 3; pp. 68–74

Smith, R. J. and Hall, T. (2018) 'Everyday territories: Homelessness, outreach work and city space', *British Journal of Sociology*, Vol. 69, No. 2, pp. 372–90; doi: 10.1111/1468-4446.12280

Snow, D. and Mulcahy, M. (2001) 'Space, politics, and the survival strategies of the homeless', *American Behavioural Scientist*, Vol. 45, No. 1, pp. 149–69; doi:

10.1177/00027640121956962

Social Bite (2017) 'Scotland's transition to rapid rehousing' (online). Available from URL: www.sleepinthepark.co.uk/sites/sleepinthepark/downloads/RRTP-Guidance.pdf (accessed 10 October 2018)

Somerville, P. (1992) 'Homelessness and the meaning of home: Rooflessness and rootlessness?', *International Journal of Urban and Regional Research*, Vol. 16, No. 4, pp. 529–39; doi: 10.1111/j.1468–2427.1992.tb00194.x

Song, S. J., Subica, A., Kaplan, C., Tol, W. and De Jong, J. (2018) 'Predicting the mental health and functioning of torture survivors', *Journal of Nervous and Mental Disease*, Vol. 206, No. 1, pp. 33–9; doi: 10.1097/NMD.0000000000000678

Sousa, C. A., Kemp, S. and El-Zuhairim, M. (2014) 'Dwelling within political violence: Palestinian women's narratives of home, mental health, and violence', *Health & Place*, Vol. 30, pp. 205–14; doi: 10.1016/j.healthplace.2014.09.005

Speer, J. (2018) 'Urban makeovers, homeless encampments, and the aesthetics of displacement', *Social & Cultural Geography*, pp. 1–21; doi: 10.1080/14649365.2018.1509115

St Mungo's (2013) *Health and Homelessness: Understanding the Costs and Role of Primary Care Services for Homeless People*, London: St Mungo's

Standing, G. (2011) *The Precariat: The Dangerous New Class*, New York:, NY Bloomsbury Academic

Starfield, B. (2012) 'Primary care: An increasingly important contributor to effectiveness, equity, and efficiency of health services', SESPAS Report 2012, *Gaceta Sanitaria*, Vol. 26, pp. 20–6

Statista (2017) 'Film industry in India: Statistics and facts' (online). Available from URL: www.statista.com/topics/2140/film-industry-in-india (accessed 11 February 2019)

Stempel, C., Sami, N., Koga, P. M., Alemi, Q., Smith, V. and Shirazi, A. (2016) 'Gendered sources of distress and resilience among Afghan refugees in northern California: Aa cross-sectional study', *International Journal of Environmental Research in Public Health*, Vol. 14, No. 25; doi: 10.3390/ijerph14010025

Stewart, W. (2018) 'FIFA World Cup: Russia denies claims that the homeless have been beaten and removed from the city streets', *Evening Standard*, 8 June. Available from URL: www.standard.co.uk/news/world/fifa-world-cup-2018-russia-denies-claims-homeless-people-have-been-beaten-and-removed-from-host-a3858551.html (accessed 12 July 2018)

Still Human Still Here (2013) 'Written evidence submitted by the Still Human Still Here coalition to the Home Affairs Committee' (online), prepared 11 October 2013. Available from URL: www.publications.parliament.uk/pa/cm201314/cmselect/cmhaff/71/71we-5.htm (accessed 14 January 2014)

Still Human Still Here (2017) 'Still human, still here' (film). Available from URL: www.amnesty.org.uk/resources/still-human-still-here-film (accessed 12 May 2017)

Story, A., Aldridge, R., Gray, T., Burridge, S. and Hayward, A. (2014) 'Influenza vaccination, inverse care and homelessness: Cross-sectional survey of eligibility and uptake during the 2011/12 season in London', *BMC Public Health*, Vol. 14, No. 44; doi: 10.1186/1471–2458–14–44

Street Soccer Scotland (2018) 'Positive change through football' (online). Available from URL: www.streetsoccerscotland.org (accessed 12 July 2018)

Streetwise Opera (2018) 'The impact of Streetwise Opera: 2017–2018' (online). Available from URL: www.streetwiseopera.org/sites/default/files/Streetwise%20Opera%20Impact%20Report%202017–2018.pdf (accessed 18 September 2018)

Stuckler, D. and Basu, S. (2013) *The Body Economic. Why Austerity Kills. Recessions, Budget Battles, and the Politics of Life and Death*, New York, NY: Basic Books

Swanson, K. (2010) *Begging as a Path to Progress: Indigenous Women and Children and the Struggle for Ecuador's Urban Spaces*, Athens, GA and London: University of Georgia Press

Taylor, D. (2009) *Underground Lives: An Investigation into the Living Conditions and Survival Strategies of Destitute Asylum Seekers in the UK*, Leeds: PAFRAS. Available from URL: www.irr.org.uk/pdf2/Underground_Lives.pdf (accessed 14 January 2014)

Taylor, D. (2017) 'High court rules more than 10,000 asylum seekers treated unfairly', *The Guardian*, 17 January. Available from URL: www.theguardian.com/uk-news/2017/jan/20/uk-high-court-rules-10000-asylum-seekers-treated-unfairly-detained-fast-track (accessed 23 June 2018)

Tomas, A. and Dittmar, H. (1995) 'The experience of homeless women: An exploration of housing histories and the meaning of home', *Housing Studies*, Vol. 10, No. 4, pp. 493–515; doi: 10.1080/02673039508720834

Townsend, M. (2017a) 'Home Office letter tells EU citizens to "go home or go elsewhere" ', *The Guardian*, 29 October. Available from URL: www.theguardian.com/uk-news/2017/oct/29/home-office-eu-citizens-leave-uk-avoid-destitution (accessed 10 December 2017)

Townsend, M. (2017b) 'Home Office used charity data map to deport rough sleepers', *The Guardian*, 19 August. Available from URL: www.theguardian.com/uk-news/2017/aug/19/home-office-secret-emails-data-homeless-eu-nationals (accessed 26 June 2018)

Travis, P. (2013) 'Immigration bill: Theresa May defends plans to create "hostile environment" ', *The Guardian*, 10 October. Available from URL: www.theguardian.com/politics/2013/oct/10/immigration-bill-theresa-may-hostile-environment (accessed 12 October 2013)

Tsemberis, S. (2010) 'Housing first: The pathways model to end homelessness for people with mental illness and addiction manual', *European Journal of Homelessness*, Vol. 5, No. 2

Tsemberis, S. and Eisenberg, R. F. (2000) 'Pathways to housing: Supported housing for street-dwelling homeless individuals with psychiatric disabilities', *Psychiatric Services*, Vol. 51, No. 4, pp. 487–93; doi: 10.1176/appi.ps.51.4.487

Tsemberis, S., Gulcur, L. and Nakae, M. (2004) 'Housing First, consumer choice, and harm reduction for homeless individuals with a dual diagnosis', *American Journal of Public Health*, Vol. 94, No. 4, pp. 651–6

Tudor Hart, J. (1972) 'The inverse care law', *The Lancet*, Vol. 297, No. 7696, pp. 405–12; doi: 10.1016/S0140-6736(71)92410-X

Tutty, L. M., Ogden, C., Giurgiu, B. and Weaver-Dunlop, G. (2013) 'I built my house of hope: Abused women and pathways into homelessness', *Violence Against Women*, Vol. 19, No. 12, pp. 1498–1517; doi: 10.1177/1077801213517514

Tweed, E., McCann, A. and Arnott, J. (2017) 'Foundations for well-being: Reconnecting public health and housing. A practical guide to improving health and reducing inequalities', Scottish Public Health Network (online). Available from URL: www.scotphn.net/wp-content/uploads/2017/02/2017_02_22-HH-Main-Report-Final-2.pdf (accessed 17 September 2018)

Tyler, I. (2006) ' "Welcome to Britain": The cultural politics of asylum', *Cultural Studies*, Vol, 9, No. 2, pp. 185–202; doi: 10.1177/1367549406063163

Tyler, I. (2013) *Revolting Subjects: Social Abjection and Resistance in Neoliberal Britain*, London: Zed Books

UN (United Nations) (2000) 'Millennium development goals' (online). Available from URL: www.un.org/millenniumgoals (accessed 8 July 2014)

UN (2016) 'Sustainable development goals: 17 goals to transform our world' (online). Available from URL: www.un.org/sustainabledevelopment/blog/2015/12/sustainable-development-goals-kick-off-with-start-of-new-year (accessed 10 February 2016)

UN (2017) 'World mortality 2017' (online). Available from URL: www.un.org/en/development/desa/population/publications/pdf/mortality/World-Mortality-2017-Data-Booklet.pdf (accessed 23 May 2018)

UNDP (United Nations Development Programme) (2015) 'Human development report: Work for human development' (online). Available from URL: http://hdr.undp.org/sites/default/files/2015_human_development_report.pdf (accesssed 13 March 2017)

UNHCR (UN High Commission for Refugees) (2016a) 'Global strategy beyond detention: Baseline report. A global strategy to support governments to end the detention of asylum-seekers and refugees. 2014–2019' (online). Available from URL: www.unhcr.org/uk/protection/detention/57b579d84/unhcr-global-strategy-beyond-detention-baseline-report.html (accessed 11 February 2019)

UNHCR (2016b) 'Global strategy beyond detention: A progress report. A global strategy to support governments to end the detention of asylum-seekers and refugees, 2014–2019' (online). Available from URL: www.unhcr.org/search?comid=57b579044&cid=49aea9390&scid=53aa926a6&tid=49ec6f172a&tags=report (accessed 27 February 2017)

UNHCR (2018) 'Global trends: Forced displacement in 2017' (online). Available from URL: www.unhcr.org/uk/statistics/unhcrstats/5b27be547/unhcr-global-trends-2017.html (accessed 23 September 2018)

UNHCR and Save the Children UK (2002) 'Sexual violence and exploitation: The experience of refugee children in Liberia, Guinea, and Sierra Leone', Women War Peace.org (UNIFEM – a Portal on Women, Peace, and Security), New York. Available from URL: www.alnap.org/help-library/sexual-violence-and-exploitation-the-experience-of-refugee-children-in-guinea-liberia (accessed 18 March 2019)

UNICEF (1989) 'United Nations Convention on the Rights of the Child' (online). Available from URL: https://downloads.unicef.org.uk/wp-content/uploads/2010/05/UNCRC_united_nations_convention_on_the_rights_ of_the_child.pdf (accessed 4 June 2015)

Unger, J. B., Kipke, M. D., Simon, T. R., Montgomery, S. B. and Johnson, C. J. (1997) 'Homeless youths and young adults in Los Angeles: Prevalence of mental health problems and the relationship between mental health and substance abuse disorders', *American Journal of Community Psychology*, Vol. 25, No. 3, pp. 371–94; doi: 10.1023/A:1024680727864

Upton, L. (2016) 'Care, control, or criminalization? Discourses on homelessness and social responses' (unpublished PhD), Norfolk, VA: Old Dominion University

Urry, J. (2007) *Mobilities*, Cambridge: Polity Press

US Department of Housing and Urban Development (2017) 'Part 1: Point-in-time estimates of homelessness', the 2017 annual homelessness assessment report (AHAR) to Congress. Available from URL: www.hudexchange.info/resources/documents/2017-AHAR-Part-1.pdf (accessed 2 June 2018)

Valentine, G. and Harris, C. (2014) 'Strivers vs skivers: Class prejudice and the demonisation of dependency in everyday life', *Geoforum*, Vol. 53, pp. 84–92; doi: 10.1016/j.geoforum.2014.02.007

Vanderbruggen, M., Phelps, J., Sebtaoui, N., Kovats, A. and Pollet, K. (2014) 'Point of no return: the futile detention of unreturnable migrants' (online). Available from URL: http://pointofnoreturn.eu (accessed 4 June 2016)

Vaughan, C., Davis, E., Murdolo, A., Chen, J., Murray, L., Block, K., Quiazon, R. and Warr, D. (2015) *Promoting Community-Led Responses to Violence Against Immigrant and Refugee Women in Metropolitan and Regional Australia: The ASPIRE Project*, State of Knowledge Paper No. 7, Sydney: Australia's National Research Organisation for Women's Safety. Available from URL: https://d2c0ikyv46o3b1.cloudfront.net/anrows.org.au/s3fs-public/12_1.2%20Landscapes%20ASPIRE%20web.pdf (accessed 11 February 2019)

Viruell-Fuentes, E. A., Miranda, P. Y. and Abdulrahim, S. (2012) 'More than culture: Structural racism, intersectionality theory, and immigrant health', *Social Science & Medicine*, Vol. 75, No. 12, pp. 2099–106; doi: 10.1016/j.socscimed.2011.12.037

Vossoughi, N., Jackson, Y., Gusler, S. and Stone, K. (2016) 'Mental health outcomes for youth living in refugee camps: A review', *Trauma, Violence & Abuse*, Vol. 19, No. 5; doi: 10.1177/1524838016673602

Wacquant, L. (2007) 'Territorial stigmatization in the age of advanced marginality', *Thesis Eleven*, Vol. 91, No. 1, pp. 66–77; doi: 10.1177/0725513607082003

Wacquant, L. (2009) *Punishing the Poor: The Neoliberal Government of Social Insecurity*, Durham: Duke University Press

Waft, C., Clark, L., Desai, M., Rabinovitz, S., Agahi, G., Calvo, R. and Hoffmann, J. (2013) 'Coming of age on the streets: Survival sex among homeless young women in Hollywood', *Journal of Adolescence*, Vol. 36, No. 6, pp. 1205–13

Waite, L., Lewis, H., Hodkinson, S. and Dwyer, P. (2015) 'Refused asylum seekers as the hyper-exploited', in Craig, G., Waite, L., Lewis, H., Skrivankova, K. (eds) (2015) *Vulnerability, Exploitation and Migrants*: Insecure work in a globalised economy. London: Palgrave Macmillan, pp. 143–57

Walby, K. and Lippert, R. (2011) 'Spatial regulation, dispersal, and the aesthetics of the city: Conservation officer policing of homeless people in Ottawa, Canada', *Antipode*, Vol. 44, No. 3, pp. 1015–33; doi: 10.1111/j.1467–8330.2011.00923.x

Wallace, R. (1990) 'Urban desertification, public health and public order: "Planned shrinkage", violent death, substance abuse and AIDS in the Bronx', *Social Science & Medicine*, Vol. 3, No. 7, pp. 801–13

Watkin, M. (2013) *Otherwise Homeless: Vehicle Living and the Culture of Homelessness*, Boulder, CO: FirstForum Press

Watson, J. (2011) 'Understanding survival sex: Young women, homelessness and intimate relationships', *Journal of Youth Studies*, Vol. 14, No. 6, pp. 639–55; doi: 10.1080/13676261.2011.588945

Watson, J. (2016) 'Gender-based violence and young homeless women: Femininity, embodiment and vicarious physical capital', *Sociological Review*, Vol. 64, No. 2, pp. 256–73; doi: 10.1111/1467–954X.12365

Watson, J. (2017) *Youth Homelessness and Survival Sex: Intimate Relationships and Gendered Subjectivities*, Abingdon: Routledge

Watson, J. and Cuervo, H. (2017) 'Youth homelessness: A social justice approach', *Journal of Sociology*, Vol. 53, No. 2, pp. 461–75; doi: 10.1177/1440783317705204

Watson, S. (2000) 'Homelessness revisited: New reflections on old paradigms', *Urban Policy and Research*, Vol. 18, No. 2, pp. 159–70; doi: 10.1080/08111140008727830

Watts, J. (2008) 'Beijing announces pre-olympic social clean-up', *The Guardian*, 23 January. Available from URL: https://www.theguardian.com/world/2008/jan/23/china.jonathanwatts (accessed 24 May 2017)

Waugh, A., Clarke A., Knowles, J. and Rowley, D. (2018) 'Health and homelessness in Scotland' (online). Available from URL: https://beta.gov.scot/binaries/content/documents/govscot/publications/research-publication/2018/06/health-homelessness-scotland/documents/00536908-pdf/00536908-pdf/govscot:document (accessed 10 October 2018)

Whitehead, M. (2007) 'A typology of actions to tackle social inequalities in health', *Journal of Epidemiology and Community Health*, Vol. 61, No. 6, pp. 473–8; doi: 10.1136/jech.2005.037242

Whitehead, M. and Doran, T. (2011) 'The north–south health divide', *British Medical Journal*, Vol. 343, No. 7794, p. 392

WHO (World Health Organization) (2008). *Closing the Gap in a Generation: Health Equity through Action on the Social Determinants of Health*, Final Report of the Commission on Social Determinants of Health, Geneva: World Health Organization. Available from URL: whqlibdoc.who.int/publications/2008/9789241563703_eng.pdf (accessed 7 April 2018)

WHO (2014) *Review of the Social Determinants and the Health Divide in the European Region: A Final Report*, London: London School of Economics

WHO (2016a) 'Global health observatory data: Healthy life-expectancy at birth' (online). Available from URL: who.int/gho/mortality_burden_disease/life_tables/hale/en (accessed 3 March 2018)

WHO (2016b) 'Global health statistics 2016: Monitoring health for the SDGs sustainable development goals' (online). Available from URL: www.who.int/gho/publications/world_health_statistics/2016/en (accessed 18 July 2018)

WHO (2017) 'Ten years in public health 2007–2017' (online). Available from URL: www.who.int/publications/10-year-review/dg-letter/en (accessed 18 July 2018)

WHO (2018a) 'Social determinants of health' (online). Available from URL: www.who.int/social_determinants/en (accessed 18 August 2018)

WHO (2018b) 'Health and sustainable development: Slum upgrading' (online). Available from URL: www.who.int/sustainable-development/cities/strategies/slum-upgrading/en (accessed 24 September 2018)

WHO (2018c) 'Constitution of WHO: Principles' (online). Available from URL: www.who.int/about/mission/en (accessed 10 October 2018)

Wilkinson, R. and Pickett, K. (2018) *The Inner Level: How More Equal Societies Reduce Stress, Restore Sanity and Improve Everyone's Well-Being*, Milton Keynes: Allen Lane

Williams, Z. (2013) 'Skivers v strivers: The argument that pollutes people's minds', *The Guardian*, 9 January. Available from URL: www.theguardian.com/politics/2013/jan/09/skivers-v-strivers-argument-pollutes (accessed 27 September 2018)

Wolf, J., Anderson, I., van den Dries, L. and Filipovič Hrast, M. (2016) 'The health of homeless women', in Mayock, P. and Bretherton, J. (2016) *Women's Homelessness in Europe*, London: Palgrave Macmillan, pp. 155–78

Wolitski, R. J., Pals, S., Kidder, D., Courtney-Quirk, C. and Holtgrave, D. (2009) 'The effects of HIV stigma on health, disclosure of HIV status, and risk behaviour of homeless and unstably housed persons living with HIV, *AIDS Behavior*, Vol. 13, No. 9, pp. 1222–32

Wolitski, R. J., Kidder, S., Pals, L., Royal, S., Aidala, A. and Stall, R. (2010) 'Randomised trial of the effects of housing assistance on the health and risk behaviours of homeless and unstably housed people living with HIV', *AIDs and Behavior*, Vol. 14, No. 3, pp. 493–503

Women's Health and Equity Consortium (2017) Available from URL: www.whec.org.uk/?page_id=306 (accessed 19 June 2018)

Woodhall-Melnik, J. and Dunn, J. (2015) 'A systematic review of outcomes associated with participation in Housing First programs', *Housing Studies*, Vol. 31, No. 3, pp. 1–18; doi: 10.1080/02673037.2015.1080816

Woodhall-Melnik, J., Hamilton-Wright, S., Daoud, N., Dunn, J. R. and O'Campo, P. (2017) 'Establishing stability: Exploring the meaning of "home" for women who have experienced intimate partner violence', *Journal of Housing and the Built Environment*, Vol. 32, pp. 253–68; doi: 10.1007/s10901-016-9511-8

World Bank (2016) 'India's poverty profile' (online). Available from URL: www.worldbank.org/en/news/infographic/2016/05/27/india-s-poverty-profile (accessed 18 July 2018)

World Bank (2018a) 'Global economic prospects: Growth-based upturn but for how long?' (online). Available from URL: https://openknowledge.worldbank.org/bitstream/handle/10986/28932/9781464811630.pdf (accessed 18 July 2018)

World Bank (2018b) 'India data' (online). Available from URL: https://data.worldbank.org/country/india (accessed 18 July 2018)

Worley, W. (2017) 'Homeless spikes installed to stop people sleeping rough in

Manchester city centre', *Independent*, 29 January. Available from URL: www. independent.co.uk/news/uk/home-news/homeless-spikes-manchester-homelessness-rough-sleeping-a7551136.html (accessed 1 August 2018)

Wright, T. (1997) *Out of Place: Homeless Mobilizations, Subcities and Contested Landscapes*, Albany, NY: State University of New York Press

Yorkshire Post (2017) 'Education "key" to escaping homelessness', *Yorkshire Post*, 15 July. Available from URL: www.yorkshirepost.co.uk/news/education-key-to-escaping-homelessness-1–8651197 (accessed 18 July 2018)

Zaretzky, K., Flatau, P., Spicer, B., Conroy, E. and Burns, L. (2017) 'What drives the high health care costs of the homeless?', *Housing Studies*, Vol. 32, No. 7, pp. 931–47

Zukin, S., Kasinitz, P. and Chen, X. (2015) (eds) *Global Cities, Local Streets*, New York, NY: Routledge

Index